John W. Nicholson

No Half Truths

Reminiscences of Life in Bristol Bay, Alaska, 1906—1995

John W. Nicholson

Line Drawings by Steve Peterson, Teacher

ISBN 0-9644809-4-8

Library of Congress Catalog Card Number: 95-70296

Copyright @ 1995 by John W. Nicholson
—First Edition—

Manufactured in the United States of America

All rights reserved. No part of this publication may be reproduced or transmitted in any form or by an means, electronic or mechanical, including photocopy, recording, or any information retrieval system without permission in writing of the author, except for short excerpts in reviews or scholarly works. Individuals desiring to order copies of this book are encouraged to contact John W. Nicholson at Box 41, Dillingham, Alaska 99576 or call (907) 842-5373.

Published by Publication Consultants
Anchorage, Alaska

Dedication

All my family, past, present, and future.
For enjoyment of memories of the past.

Table of Contents

Preface	7
Acknowledgments	9
Map of Nushagak Bay	11
1 The Early Days	13
2 Life at Clark's Point	21
3 Old Dillingham	25
4 Territorial Commissioner	31
5 Kanakanak Hospital	33
6 Trapping	37
7 Hunting	45
8 Dog Team Travel	49
9 Guiding	55
10 Road Construction	59
11 Taxi Service	63
Photo Album	65
12 Social Life	97
13 Airplanes	101
14 Alaska Territorial Guard	105
15 Reindeer Herding	109
16 Commercial Salmon Fishing	113
17 More Sailboat and Other Fishing Stories	125
18 Fishermen Unions	133
19 Visit to the Lower Forty Eight	137
20 Marriages	141
21 Skating at 84 Years of Age	149
22 Alcoholic Days	151
Index	156

Preface

Our father, John W. Nicholson, is one of the few old-timer's left in Bristol Bay. He was born in Clark's Point, Alaska, in 1906. Through the depression and two world wars, he sailed Nushagak Bay in a small, wooden fishing boat, carving a living by gillnetting salmon. Muttering a hearty "mush" to his barking leader, Dad, clad in a heavy parky and cotton gloves, rode on dog team sled runners for thousands of miles. Using homemade snowshoes, he plowed across mountain-high snow drifts. For decades, with ice pick in hand, he hacked holes in the ice to place beaver snares. He subsisted off a land which abounds in ptarmigan, spruce hen, and water fowl. Luckily, falling a moose or caribou, he fed his family. (Dad has many children and grandchildren who live in Dillingham.)

Civic minded, during the long, cold winter months of the territorial era, he mailed letters to the newspaper editor advocating Alaska statehood.

In April of 1988, Dad was awarded the Bristol Bay Senior Fishermen Award in recognition of his many years of commitment to commercial fishing and his contribution to the promotion and growth of the Bristol Bay salmon fishery. In April 1992, Governor Walter Hickel recognized Dad for his ice-skating exploits as ". . . one whose dedication to fitness and a can-do spirit are what make Alaska great!" In April 1995, the Alaska State Legislature recognized him as an elder in Bristol Bay, which helped him to celebrate his 89th birthday. Today, our dad still remains active in his subsistence pursuits near Kanakanak, and he's still skating.

Here, our dad presents his No Half Truths, which are personal glimpses of life in Bristol Bay from 1906 to the present. He took extra pains to assure accuracy in regard to historical information.

Important to the region is the significance of the commercial fishing industry, which employs most people on a seasonal basis. Glimpses into health, transportation, education, and cultural history of the area is also valuable, since few historical documents deal with events and life in this area. Although this is not a scholarly work, since it has been written for his family and relatives, our dad shares a window into a past that many would like to know more about. The reader will undoubtably agree our father's reminiscences help us to better understand a facet of Bristol Bay's unique, historical heritage.

His Family
1995

Acknowledgments

I thank my sister, Emma Raven, of Sunnyvale, California, for providing financial support, which made publishing of this book possible. Special thanks goes to my son, William Nicholson, who did the lion's share of the work by typing and editing this manuscript, and making it ready for publishing.

Steve Peterson deserves credit for drawings he provided for this work.

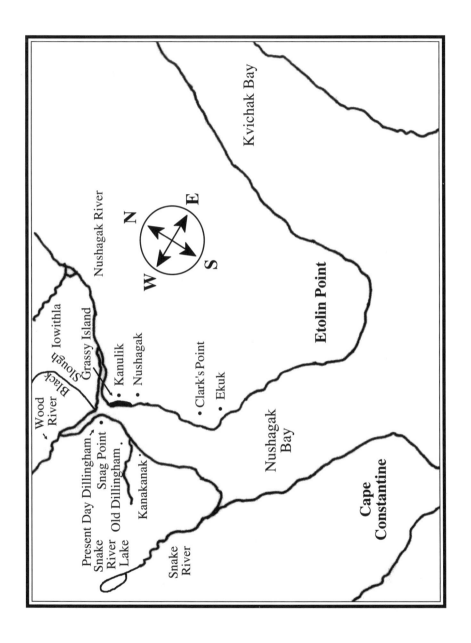

Chapter One

The Early Days

My name is John W. Nicholson. I was born on April 14, 1906, at Clark's Point, Alaska. I am the eldest of ten children. My father, Hans P. Nicholson, was born in Copenhagen, Denmark. As a young boy, he jumped aboard a merchant ship, sailed throughout the world, and eventually wound up on the west coast of America. After his arrival, he heard about the silver salmon runs in Bristol Bay, Alaska, and the development of the salmon packing companies. These packing companies held promise of new work. He arrived in Bristol Bay before the turn of the Twentieth Century. Taking a liking to this new country, he decided to stay in the area. When I was born, he was working as the winter watchman for the Alaska Packers Cannery at Clark's Point.

Dad worked at Clark's Point until 1911. In 1912, he began a salmon saltry at Snake River, where he installed two fish traps. These traps were extremely efficient, so my father hired a small crew to scoop out the fish. He used a power boat for towing a miniature, flat scow for carrying fish. The workers would load the scow, and the salmon were transported to shore to be split and processed. The fish were then laid individually inside a big, round tank with rock salt covering the layers of salmon backs and bellies. After laying in the big tank for several days, the brine was drained. The fish were then taken out of the tanks and layered into two hundred pound barrels. Each barrel had a small hole on top, and was used to pour fresh brine into the barrel. The barrels were sealed, and the salted salmon was ready for shipment to market. Although this operation had great potential, the summer of 1913 was the last time my father operated the saltry. He was forced to quit because the market was poor for salt salmon; possibly the biggest reason was that he did not have the financial backing to continue. The fall of 1913, the last of my father's salt salmon was loaded on the Ekuk Haller Cannery's sailing ship for shipment to Seattle.

While my father operated the saltry at Snake River, I saw an impressive sight. Gazing across the tundra from Snake River toward the east side of Nushagak Bay, three-masted, wooden sailing ships, freighters from Seattle, were anchored off the little communities of Clark's Point and Ekuk. Moored alongside them were smaller steamers that earlier towed them into Nushagak Bay. The steamers were silently waiting to tow the freighters back out through the shallow water and around the many sandbars to the open, ominous waters of the Bering Sea.

Our family wintered at Kanulik, better known as Carmel, during 1911 and 1912. I saw the empty, ghost-like buildings of the Moravian Mission, the Alaska Packers Salmon Cannery, and a little hospital building serving the Native people and seasonal cannery workers. The winter of 1913, we lived at the Ekuk Haller Cannery. Being industrious by nature, my father was successful in being hired as Haller's winter watchman.

Experiencing a growing desire to fish commercially, I felt the easiest way I could make money was to setnet for salmon. I did this for the first time when I was eleven years old. It was hard work even for a grown up. I liked the work, so I continued to fish each summer

The Early Days

from 1917 to 1920 on Ekuk's gravel beach. My father encouraged me to fish. He knew the value of good, honest work. When I was twelve years old, he built a small, wooden skiff for me. I was extremely happy to own this little vessel. It was small, but it could carry a load.

When the wind was calm or when the waters were rough, I picked my setnet, which was often full of fish. With growing pride, I would row my new skiff, loaded with salmon, up the Nushagak Bay to sell my catch. Soon, I was at the buyer's station located on the cannery dock. Once, when the bay was too rough to row my skiff to the dock, someone from the cannery crew loaned me a big, two-wheeled fish cart to transport the fish. Not wanting to do all the work myself, I hitched up a seven-dog team to the cart, and delivered my catch.

I remember once, when I was hauling a load of salmon, I drove the dogs through a warehouse. The tow line got wrapped around a couple of wooden poles. What a mess it turned out to be! I had a problem straightening out the dog team. While I was doing this, some people overheard me cursing like the older men sometimes did. Soon after, I was able to drive through the warehouse and, with satisfaction, make it to the buying station. The fish delivered meant only a few cents, but ultimately, it added up. I hoped I didn't have to give it all to my dad, because I worked long and hard for it!

My brothers, sisters, and I understood Dad was well respected in Ekuk. He was opinionated as to what we could or couldn't do. It was about this time that Dad gave me the responsibility of raising the American flag by rope and pulley whenever any sailing ship or steamer from the Lower Forty-eight States came up the Nushagak. The arriving vessels usually flew an American flag when they entered the bay. The custom was, when a ship sailed past Ekuk, we would lower and raise the stars and stripes at least three times. This signified a hello or salute. The ship's captain responded by raising, lowering, and then raising their flag, too.

Suddenly one day, without any warning, an ocean-going, three-masted sailing ship approached Ekuk. I was so excited I raised the flag upside down. When Dad saw the flag flying upside down, he got angry and bawled me out. It seems that flying the flag upside down was a distress signal. By the time I was able to get the flag down, attach it correctly, and then raise it again, the ship was past Ekuk and out of sight.

Since my father sailed with merchant ships throughout the world, he had become acquainted with many of the sailing ship captains. He usually went out of his way to visit new captains upon their arrival. He joked and shared stories of the old sailing days in different lands and circumstances. I am also certain he mentioned my flag-raising mishap and joked about it too.

Sailing by ocean-going ship from San Francisco to Ekuk took about twenty-eight to thirty days, and sometimes more, depending on weather and sea conditions. Along with the supplies for the cannery, Outside fishermen were transported to Bristol Bay. They would help with sailing the ship. They pulled themselves quickly, hand over hand, up and down the ropes to secure the sails. Each spring, I watched fishermen, cannery workers, and the China gang disembarking from the schooners.

During winter months before World War One, Dad took my sister, Emma, and I to the village of Nushagak to live with our grandma, Natalia Clark. This is where I went to school. I enjoyed living at Nushagak. It was the main town on the Nushagak River. It had a trading post constructed out of milled lumber. An impressive looking Russian Orthodox Church stood out on the hillside. Nushagak was also called Fort Alexander. Walking through this site, I remember seeing a small cannon near a flag pole.

One day at Nushagak, my grandmother, Natalia said, "There's a ptarmigan outside, not too far from the house! Take the single-barrel, twelve-gauge shotgun!" I was hesitant at first, since I was only nine years old and had never shot a shotgun before. She said, "Try it." So, I walked outside, pointed the barrel toward the ptarmigan, and pulled the trigger. The blast knocked me backward. I must have closed my eyes when I pulled the trigger. Realizing my grandmother was behind me, I asked her where the ptarmigan went. She said, "You killed it!" After a short search, I found it laying behind a little pile of snow; my first ptarmigan! I'd used a reloadable brass shotgun shell, which was

The Early Days

probably overcharged. That's what knocked me backwards. At that time, there were no paper or plastic shotgun shells.

When the Christmas holiday arrived, I was selected by the Russian Orthodox priest as one of the boys to ring the church bells. Ringing the church bells was a Russian religious custom which brought more of a holiday spirit to all of us at Nushagak.

At Nushagak, my teacher's name was Red McClain. His two boys were my close friends. One day, to everyone's complete surprise, he killed his wife. After that, Tom Padden became my teacher. He taught me reading, writing, and arithmetic, for which I am still thankful.

John W. Clark, a well-known local figure, was my grandfather on my mother's side. He operated the Nushagak trading post for Alaska Commercial Company. From the trading post, he sent Natives across the Alaska Peninsula to the Pacific Ocean to hunt sea otters. He became the owner of the trading post and continued to operate it. As a tribute, Lake Clark was named after him because of his survey and guiding work. Clark's Point was named after him for his important contributions toward the establishment of the community.

Feodora Clark Nicholson, my mother, was just six years old when Grandfather Clark died on December 8, 1896. After the funeral, he was buried on top of Nushagak hill above the old Fort Alexander site. Today, his heavy marble head stone can be found, although brush has overgrown the cemetery. When my grandfather died, my mother and her two sisters received an inheritance of $10,000 each. It is unknown how much money my grandmother received when Mr. Mittendorf (first name unknown) purchased the trading post, but it was a significant amount.

Although Mr. Mittendorf now owned my grandfather's store, it didn't change my interest in visiting the store. From Grandma Clark's house, I walked uphill to the store and bought packaged corn flakes, a cereal I especially liked to eat. One day, when a supply ship arrived, it dropped anchor off Nushagak. Mr. Mittendorf received a large supply of hardware and goods, which was barged to shore. Shortly after, I saw bananas hanging in the store. I ran to Grandma's front room and begged for some money. My craving wasn't satisfied until

I ate a whole bunch of bananas. The store didn't stock much fresh fruit, because it would not keep. The fresh fruit would soon be sold out, and I'd have to wait another long year for bananas.

My grandmother remarried a man by the name of Hans Hoidahl. He built me a small, wooden basket sled with long handles. These oak handle bars pointed straight back from the bow of the sled and were used to help steer the sled. I invited the two McClain boys over. We harnessed three sled dogs to the tow line. Our intention was to ride two miles away and back. While I was on the sled runners and yelling at the team to go faster, I slipped. I broke a front tooth perfectly in half on the oak handle bars of the sled. This was painful.

After a couple of years, a medical doctor from the Kanakanak Hospital was able to work on my teeth. The doctor installed a golden crown over the broken tooth, which I wore for several years. Later, when I visited Anchorage, I had additional dental work done. After my teeth were x-rayed, the dentist mentioned that the crown and the half-tooth should be taken out because of an infection in the tooth root. The crown and tooth were extracted. I kept the crown for several decades. When my son, William, saw the golden crown, he asked to keep it. I said, "Keep it!". I guess he wanted to find out what it was worth from an assayer in Anchorage.

The problems with my teeth lasted many years. At Ekuk, when I was in my thirties, several of my teeth decayed. I remember suffering terribly from a toothache that lasted for eight long days. I would receive a little relief when I held cold water in my mouth. The pain got so bad that I told myself, "When I find a dentist, all of my teeth will come out!". On the eighth day, I flew to Anchorage. I told the dentist I wanted all of my teeth pulled out. He asked me why. I told him simply, "They're causing me too much suffering, and where I live there are no dentists." After a thorough examination, the dentist told me I still had fourteen good teeth. I insisted he pull them all out. The dentist extracted them—the good with the bad. As a result, my gums were torn. The teeth had hooks at the roots that tore up the gum tissue as they were removed. Months later, he made me a set of new false teeth. When I tried them out, I found that I could chew tough meat,

The Early Days

at last.

Over time, my gums developed toughness, possibly helped by my snuff chewing habit. A pinch of Copenhagen snuff was always in my mouth. The snuff worked its way under the plates. I had the habit of taking the false teeth out when I wanted a fresh pinch of snuff. Once, when I was doing this, I dropped them on the ground. They broke in two. I had to have another set made, which I wore for several years. Finally at an older age, I got tired of putting them in and out of my mouth. So, I quit wearing them. Now, when I want to chew dry salmon, I pull out my carpenter's hammer and pound it on the corner of my kitchen table. This way, the food is soft enough.

Chapter Two

Life at Clark's Point

In the autumn of 1920, when I was fourteen years old, our family moved from Ekuk to Clark's Point. Clark's Point, a community located alongside the Nushagak Bay, is several miles south of Nushagak and a mile north of Ekuk. Dad was hired as winter watchman for Alaska Packers Cannery.

The next summer, I continued to setnet for salmon on the sloped, gravel beach near Clark's Point Cannery. One day, the superintendent for Alaska Packers Cannery offered me a full-sized twenty eight-foot sailboat. So, I ran down to pick my most recent catch out of the setnet, delivered the salmon and prepared to sail with the men. Soon, I slowly and silently sailed from the Clark's Point pile-driven dock to driftnet on Nushagak Bay. Earlier, I had spent many hours watching the fishermen sail their boats, so sailing was natural for me. At fifteen years of age, I entered the ranks of adults who made money drift fishing for salmon.

My father wrote to Juneau, the Territorial Capitol, requesting a school be started at Clark's Point. He wanted his children to be close to home, instead of sending them to Nushagak each winter. Alaska Packers Cannery at Clark's Point had two vacant buildings. One became a school, and the other became a teacher's quarters.

My father also wrote to Juneau seeking a permit to trap young red foxes before the trapping season opened, then breed them. He was successful in obtaining a special permit to apprehend three pair of red fox, the first year, and another three pair, the second year. I helped my father catch the foxes on the Clark's Point Bluff. We used small, steel traps (# 0), to keep from hurting the foxes' feet.

Southwestern Alaska was a small place during the early 1900s, and news traveled quickly. A game warden from Bethel on the Kuskokwim River heard rumors that my father was fox trapping out of season, and soon traveled from Bethel to Clark's Point by dog team to investigate the report. It was a long and dangerous trip through the mountains and over the coastal area. When the warden arrived, Dad showed him the fox permit from Juneau. Dad must have enjoyed his coffee with the stranger from Bethel. We found out that the fox wouldn't breed, so there was no use keeping them. They were killed when the skins were prime. Sadly, fox farming at Clark's Point was a failure.

One day, I took a walk down a short gravel road with some of the employees from the cannery cookhouse. We saw men digging in the graveyard with people watching on the side. The cannery graveyard was located a little way off the traffic area. Walking closer, we found the diggers were Chinese. We asked who the grave was for. Responding, one of the Chinese said, "After twenty years in the ground, we dig up Chinese bones, put them in wooden boxes, and ship the bones back to China." After viewing the human remains, back at the cookhouse, some of the cookhouse workers lost their appetite. I was okay.

Some of the Chinese men had long, braided hair hanging down to their waist. They worked along with Mexicans as slime workers, heading and gutting fish for the cannery. Later, when we moved from Clark's Point to Kanakanak, my mother knew some Chinese were buried near the riverbank at Kanakanak. These Chinese died while

Life at Clark's Point

working at Bradsford Cannery, a cannery located on the river bank one quarter mile north of the hospital at Kanakanak. Over the years, some of these graves washed away because of erosion. In the 1960s, after I arrived home at Kanakanak from commercial fishing, my wife told me there was a human head lying near her subsistence gillnet on the high-water mark. When I walked down to look, I couldn't find it. Someone had picked it up and buried it. On a separate occasion, someone found a human head with a long braid and hung it on a wall off the beach, near my wife's subsistence site. A magistrate in Dillingham heard about it. He instructed someone to bury it.

One day, at the Clark's Point fish dock, several workers were busy sliming salmon. A Mexican and an old, gray-haired Chinese man began to argue. The Chinese man was boiling mad and held a long fish pew in his short arms. He deliberately attempted to stab the sharp-pointed steel pew into the Mexican's chest. At the same time, the Mexican attempted to hack the Chinese man with a butcher knife. I thought to myself, "They are going to kill one another!" Thankfully, other Mexican and Chinese workers appeared, pulled them apart, and helped to cool them off.

As a teenager at Clark's Point, I looked forward to the spring arrival of schooners. I enjoyed watching new people come ashore from large, wooden ships anchored off Clark's Point. When Outside fishermen, Chinese gang, sprinkled with Mexicans arrived, it was a relief to see them. We saw very few people during winter months. Also, with the arrival of the ships, the Alaska Packers Cannery store would receive their supplies. I knew there would be a shipment of bottled soda pop and brightly wrapped candy. When I saw the pop bottles and candy on the shelves, my mouth watered. If I had any loose change in my pocket, I'd buy what I wanted. The pop and candy did not last long, just like the fresh fruit at Nushagak Trading Post.

Chapter Three

Old Dillingham

In the fall of 1925, our family moved from Clark's Point to a location one half mile north of Kanakanak hospital. Dad wanted to retire from working at the Clark's Point Salmon Cannery. He knew that Kanakanak had a government hospital and a Territorial school, which was placed in a beautiful setting. When we arrived on the beach below Kanakanak hospital, I walked up to the high bluff north of Bradsford Creek. Glancing from the high bluffs, Nushagak Bay appeared wide toward Grassy Island and not too far off to the northeast, the mouth of the Nushagak River and Wood River showed. A tree-line with birch and willow brush dominated by spruce trees was evident, especially to the northwest. This tree area covered many square miles. Looking north, high foothills and small mountains provided a sense of openness and grandeur to the setting. When we reached our property, Dad showed us where we could grow a good crop of potatoes and vegetables.

After moving to what would be later known as Dillingham, my

father opened up a general merchandise and grocery store. The store was located about a quarter of a mile above Bradsford creek, across the gully, and due north from the Bureau of Indian Affairs hospital. The store soon flourished. It served the area for many years. Children from the Kanakanak orphanage waded through Bradsford creek when the tide was out, and walked up the steep hill just to buy candy and other goodies at the store. Upriver trappers stopped by to buy their winter supplies. With dad's gas powered boat, I towed several of their un-motorized poling boats above the tidal waters on the Nushagak River. Poling their small wooden boats with long sticks or narrow poles, the muscular trappers pushed themselves, sometimes over a hundred miles upriver.

The trapper's boats were built long and narrow, so they could easily pole them against the strong Nushagak River current. Later, trappers bought outboard motors and attached them to the stern of their boats. Many times, the motors would quit running. Disappointed, the men once again would pole themselves upriver with great determination.

The Nushagak and Mulchatna trappers were a hardy lot. They made their living by trapping fur bearing animals. Some suffered from cabin fever. After spring breakup, they traveled down river, partied for a while and then found work at the canneries or if they were lucky, they crewed or captained fishing sailboats. In the fall months, they purchased their winter supplies and returned upriver.

The winter of 1926 was very mild. All winter long, when it snowed, it would soon melt away. Throughout the entire trapping season, I ran my nine dog team over bare tundra to check my fox sets. Early morning frost on the ground made sledding easier. I directed my lead dog with a gee or haw to go through the ponds and small lakes that were frozen. This made traveling quicker. I made a trip over to Kulukuk, near Togiak, where there was a Native village. A Bureau of Indian Affairs school was located at the head of Kulukuk Bay on the northwest side. While traveling along the north shore of Kulukuk, I noticed that the Natives recently dug up cockle clams. Kulukuk Bay was open which was very unusual. Natives lived here because of the

Old Dillingham

abundance of berries, fish from the water, water fowl, the clam beds, ptarmigan, and domesticated reindeer. Due to a sickness, or a curse by a shaman, and among other reasons, but surely because of interest in moving closer to the canneries and hospital at Kanakanak, the Kulukuk village was abandoned several years later.

During the first week in April, the mailman left Dillingham by dog team for Kanatak located east of the Alaska Peninsula on Shelikof Strait opposite Kodiak. At Kanatak, he picked up the mail bound for Dillingham. He returned with the mail by powerboat as the ice in the rivers and creeks went out early. After its arrival on May 18th, the mail boat anchored offshore at Kanakanak and the biggest snowstorm for that winter arrived. By evening though, the snow began to melt off.

Before the flood of 1929, I purchased an Indian motorcycle. There was an old man by the name of Herman Schroeder who was very inventive. I asked him to make me a special ski to take the place of the front wheel of my motorcycle. He also made skis for both sides of the rear wheel with springs, so that when there is a low spot between the skis, the rear wheel still had traction. In the fall of 1929, my dad had plans to start a second store over at Koggiung on the Kvichak River. He wanted me to help get the store operating. I loaded my motorcycle in a boat with the newly installed skis so I could travel back to Kanakanak during the winter. The motorcycle was loaded in the stern of a double-ender sailboat where dad also packed and piled an enormous amount of store supplies. Dad's power boat, an old wooden planked Southeastern Troller was also heavily loaded with store supplies. Before leaving we covered the store items with a heavy green canvas.

After leaving Kanakanak with the sailboat in tow, we anchored out for one night at Queen Slough, located next to Clark's Point. Late the next afternoon, we left Queen Slough after the flood tide. Dad's power boat slowly towed the loaded sailboat, first in a southerly and then southeast direction. When we approached Cape Etolin, my father's usually confident face began to frown. I was more anxious than my father as I eyed the sky. The rough waters and the waves began splashing over the bow and then the entire vessel. Our small vessels ran into a wind storm that soon increased to a gale force storm with winds up to at least fifty miles an hour. For several hours, we bucked into the strong winds and sharp waves topped with white wash in dwindling day light. During the night, the sailboat began leaking and capsized. With the floundering sailboat still in tow, it took us about twenty-two hours from Queen Slough to arrive Naknek, located on the upper end of Naknek/Kvichak Bay. This trip usually takes seven to eight hours under good sea conditions.

After arrival at the Naknek dock, we righted the capsized boat. Since my motorcycle was not tied down in the stern of the boat, it probably was dumped near Cape Etolin. Only a couple of brooms, which were jammed between the seats, were the only supplies left on the boat. On the next tide, my dad and I traveled up the Naknek River to Savonoska. At Savonoska, we carried the remaining store supplies to a local Native whom we trusted. He would sell the merchandise. There were not enough supplies to begin a new store, so this was the end of dad's dreams for a second store. We left the sailboat in Naknek and went home with the Southeast Troller.

My father was postmaster at Dillingham. He used a building next to his store for the mail business. In order to have a name for the U.S. Postal Service, the name of Dillingham was taken for the small community. The post office building was small, but it was usable by the residents. It served its purpose well. Later, because of other time consuming activities, my father relinquished his postmaster position. In 1931, Margaret Salazar, a doctor's wife from the hospital, took over the post office duties.

In the late 1930s, the Dillingham post office was relocated to Snag Point about five miles north of Dillingham. Snag Point was renamed Dillingham with the arrival of the post office. I was told that a white trapper arrived from upriver, saw some snags on the gravel beach below the Native village of Choggiung and named the village Snag Point. Snag Point was called Choggiung by the Natives. It was originally a Native community. Incidentally, it is still called the Choggiung voting precinct.

Currently, the community of Dillingham has grown to a popula-

Old Dillingham

tion approaching 2500 people with new families moving in all the time. It is designated as a first-class city and has an elementary school, a middle/high school, and an University of Alaska Rural extension center. One prominent business is the Peter Pan Seafood plant, which used to be called Pacific American Fisheries (PAF). The city government is housed in the old, but renovated elementary school building.

At the original Dillingham near Kanakanak, my father remained active on the school board where he was a prominent figure. There were many mix ups, as the school freight from the lower 48 states destined for Old Dillingham wound up in New Dillingham and vice versa. In order to keep the school freight separate, dad renamed Old Dillingham to Kanakanak, a Native village south of Old Dillingham. No one lived in that Native village anymore. Many of you probably don't know it, but you can spell Kanakanak backwards or forward. I continue to live there. My post office mail continues to arrive by air in new Dillingham or Dillingham as we currently prefer to call it.

Originally, the downtown Dillingham business center was very swampy. Two inch by twelve inch wooden planks were laid for sidewalks from house to house and business to business. Plank walks also were constructed towards and around the PAF Cannery. With improvements in drainage, hauling in large amounts of gravel over the years, and the recent paving of the downtown area, the main business area is now very dry.

I have seen a lot of changes in Dillingham over the years. It was interesting to view the changes first hand. The community of Nushagak was a main trading center. People arrived from around the Bristol Bay region to visit. Nushagak had a post office, which received mail from a mail boat that laid at anchor off Nushagak. Nushagak possessed two important salmon canneries called Northwestern and Libby, McNeill and Libby. The two canneries, torn down decades ago, today host several setnetters who live in small summer cottages on the original site.

New names replaced old names. For example, Squaw Creek was once called Beauty Creek, named by an old man who used to live there. Before him, a fellow named Andrew built a cabin there, so many called the creek, Andrew's Creek. The name Beauty Creek did not last long. Someone came up with the name Squaw Creek. A hill south of Squaw Creek toward Kanakanak was originally called Klondike Hill. Again this was because a man by the name of Klondike built a small cabin on it. The creek immediately below it was called Klondike Creek. Later, a man staked a Native allotment on this hill and built a small cabin there. The residents began to call it, Big Foot's Hill, which it is still called today.

Dad never lost his bug for fox farming, so he wanted to try it again. This time, he tried the fur business at Kanakanak in back of his residence. He ordered two pairs of silver grays from a federal marshal who had a fox ranch in Kodiak, Alaska. The marshal shipped the four foxes on the mail boat. Before they arrived we built the fox pens. We kept the foxes for three years, but again to our dismay, they wouldn't breed.

I discovered that the female foxes were shy, kind of scared, and the males weren't afraid. When we fed the foxes, the males would put their paws up on our bodies, and the females wouldn't. The best we could do was to coax the females close by. Finally, one of them died. So we killed the other three and skinned them for their fur. That was the end of our big fox farming dreams of riches. While we had the foxes, we were glad that the orphanage children could stop by and look at them, sort of like going to a zoo for them.

Chapter Four

Territorial Commissioner

Dad was always busy. Because of his preference for an active life-style, the local people called him "High-Powered Nicholson." Significant to our family and the region, he was appointed Territorial Commissioner by a judge. He performed well in this position.

Before statehood, commercial salmon management was controlled by the United States Bureau of Fisheries. Several fishermen who setnetted on Ekuk Beach began fishing before an announced salmon opening. When they were apprehended by a patrol officer, they were brought before my father for trial. Some fishermen harvested only a few fish, others had a lot of fish. Dad would fine each one for the number of fish they had on hand. Salmon at this time brought nineteen cents each, so their fines were small. Since statehood in 1959, fishing illegally is very serious. For serious offenses, such as repeated fishing over the line offenses, the Alaska Department of Fish and Game Public Safety Division, can seize their fish boats. Some of the seized boats were sold at auction.

One fishing season, the superintendent for Wood River Cannery was extremely worried during a heavy run of salmon. The China gang was threatening to strike. The superintendent sent for Dad to speak to the Chinese leadership at the bunk house. The superintendent introduced my father as "The Commissioner." On this occasion, he told them if the strike occurred, thousands of valuable salmon will lie rotting on the dock. The cannery would lose a lot of money and their salaries would suffer. What really impacted their thinking was that if the strike occurred, their salaries would be cut drastically, especially if they stopped working during the peak of the salmon run. After my father's speech, all talk of striking was quelled.

Another time at the Ekuk Cannery, the superintendent got word the China gang was stealing canned salmon, so he sent for Dad. This happened just before the gang was to leave Ekuk for the States. The canning season was finished. My father told them, "If you don't return the canned salmon, some of you will have to go to jail!" I saw several members of the China gang rushing to their living quarters. They came right back. Some of them had only a few one-pound cans in their arms. I noticed one person, with a whole case of salmon, looked rather sheepish.

During the 1930s, it was rumored that an upriver Native named Klutak was a murderer and on the loose. Whenever someone wound up missing up the Nushagak or Mulchatna Rivers, Klutak received the blame. One day, Klutak was traveling on the upper Nushagak River. He saw men camping on the gravel beach, with a tent against the willow brush. He stopped to pay a friendly visit or to ask them for something. In spite of no real evidence, but being a suspect, the men held him prisoner. While the other two men made a side trip, one man was left to guard Klutak. The guard was careless and Klutak killed him. Later, Dad had to accompany the Federal Marshal upriver to hold an inquest. This was when Klutak disappeared.

Chapter Five

Kanakanak Hospital

The first hospital was located at Carmel (Kanulik) at the Moravian Mission. Doctor Romig, the first physician to live there year-round, served the people of the area. After 1906, the Moravian Mission at Carmel ceased to exist. The Moravians left and centered their work in the Kuskokwim region. A man obtained approval to tear down the buildings at the mission station. With some of the materials, he built a house that still stands. It is located near Squaw Creek in Dillingham.

Of historic importance, in 1918, the United States was hit by the Spanish Flu. In the spring of 1919, the flu nearly killed all the Native elders living around the Nushagak Bay area. The Native children seemed to fight off the flu better than their parents. As a result, there were many orphans when the flu epidemic ended. The federal government examined the situation, primarily due to the influence of Judge Wickersham. The result was a newly constructed orphanage near the hospital at Kanakanak. There are still a few people around who lived in this orphanage. This building was abandoned in the thirties. After the closure of the orphanage, several years later, some of the orphans married locally. Others moved to other communities.

When we moved to Old Dillingham in 1925, Kanakanak Hospital operated out of a school house that was not in use (this was the original hospital or clinic opened by the Bureau of Indian Affairs (BIA) in 1909, following the departure of the Moravian missionaries in 1906). Several years later, in 1932, the building caught fire and burned completely down. At the time of the hospital fire, the orphanage was already abandoned. It was not fit to use as a hospital. Instead, the orphanage staff's living quarters became the new replacement hospital.

A new hospital or general medical center was finally built in 1941. After the commercial fishing season, I helped build the structure over a period of four months. I was hired as a laborer, but the construction boss put me to work as a journeyman carpenter.

During the spring of 1985, construction of a new, modern hospital began. It was dedicated on November 20, 1986. The new hospital is connected to the older hospital by hallways built during the war. The older hospital rooms are now mainly used as office space.

The federal government used a supply ship named the Boxer which, each summer, brought supplies for the hospital at Kanakanak. The Boxer carried a small scow on deck. The scow was lowered by winch alongside the anchored vessel. Once alongside, the scow was loaded. The government usually hired my father's Southeast Troller to tow the scow to the beach for off-loading.

Dad also contracted out a Fordson tractor and a four-wheeled wagon. These hauled the freight up to the hospital on top of the hill. The freight was then stored in a building near the old orphanage building. Those days, the hospital heating system was fueled by coal. The Boxer carried hundreds of one hundred twenty five-pound sacks of coal. Once, they were hauled up to the storage house, I would pile them, sack by sack, like stair steps to the top of the peaked roof. When I was finished, my face was black from coal dust.

The hospital in 1925 had one resident doctor and a nurse. A Native

Kanakanak Hospital

woman worked as a helper, which included interpreter duties. There were no powered washing machines, so the nurse and the helper did the washing by hand. Few patients stayed in the hospital. Actually, the Natives were superstitious and afraid to go to the hospital. Many had more faith in their medicine man. Many Natives contracted white man diseases and died of tuberculosis. Oftentimes, Natives lay dying in crudely improvised tents outside the hospital. The doctor and nurse could only try to make them comfortable. The only medicine used were pain killers, a form of aspirin.

Since it was a BIA hospital, for a time, the white population did not receive the services of the doctor or nurse. Often, when a doctor was not available, the nurse had to fill in. Undoubtedly, some white individuals would have died if someone didn't diagnose the illnesses and prescribe the medicines. According to the ethics of the medical profession, only a doctor can diagnose illnesses, then prescribe medicine, or perform surgery. Many years later, a public health station was established at Dillingham to service the non-Natives.

The new hospital, constructed in 1941, was clean and orderly. It had its own electricity generation plant. Furnaces were installed for heating purposes. Furnace oil was supplied from Seattle. Later, additional nurses were hired and new, improved health-related equipment installed. Health services improved greatly.

Today, Kanakanak has one of the most modern hospitals in the state. Robert Clark, the current Executive Director of the hospital, is doing a fine job running the hospital. The hospital is operated by the Bristol Bay Area Health Corporation (BBAHC), a private nonprofit Native organization which was incorporated in the State of Alaska in June 1973. This organization's purpose is "... to manage and develop regional services and programs that directly affect the health and well-being of the Native residents of the Bristol Bay region. Governed by a Board of Director's consisting of one representative from each of the thirty-two communities in the region, BBAHC provides a wide array of primary, preventive, and educational health care services, including community and mental health services." By 1987, according to their reports, BBAHC became the largest employer in the region. By

1993, the Corporation employed approximately three hundred people with an operating budget of over fourteen million dollars.

Chapter Six

 # Trapping

During the winter of 1925-1926, I ran a fox trap line by dog team from Kanakanak south to Coffee Point. From Coffee Point, I turned inland toward Snake River, and then I returned in a circle back to Kanakanak and Old Dillingham. This way, I was able to check the fox sets going out and coming back. I averaged about eighteen to twenty fox a year for several years. Red fox skins were worth around seventeen to nineteen dollars each. After World War Two, the skins dropped to three or four dollars a pelt. A few years later, red fox skins became fashionable, and prices soared to eighty to one hundred dollars per pelt. I had a dandy red fox skin, for which I received one hundred and fifty dollars.

Beaver trapping season was closed for several years and reopened in 1927. The reason for the closure was due to a decimated beaver population. The first time I went beaver trapping was in the spring of 1928. I agreed to trap with a young Eskimo by the name of Steve Kevik. The previous year, he'd good experience trapping the Iowithla

River, a branch of the Nushagak. First, I hauled a skiff up to Lewis Point, ten or twelve miles north of Dillingham. I planned to use it to return to Dillingham after spring breakup. Then, we went home and waited for beaver season to open in April.

My father, mushing his dog team, carried Steve, myself and our supplies to the Iowithla. We arrived after dark and pitched a ten by twelve foot tent. My father stayed the night. He left for home the next morning. Much snow and ice remained on the ground while we trapped by foot for the next four weeks.

One day, I went snowblind in my right eye. I forgot to take along my snow glasses. The bright, spring sunlight bouncing off the snow was beautiful, but painful. My eye was miserable until I covered it with a red handkerchief.

While I was checking my beaver sets near a beaver dam, about five miles from the camp, I broke through thin ice. It was extremely cold. I was up to my armpits in water and ice. After I crawled out of the water, Steve and I quickly gathered sticks of wood. We started a fire to dry my clothes. While I was holding my pants over the fire to dry, some 22-caliber bullets dropped into the fire. Suddenly I heard gunshots. Startled, I turned away from the fire. The first thing that entered my mind was that Klutak was shooting at me. Klutak was by then, a presumed crazy Native who roamed the tundra. Some people blamed him for the disappearance of several white trappers up the Nushagak River. Fred Hatfield, another trapper, later wrote of Klutak in his book—a best seller called North of the Sun. Hatfield claims in his book that he poisoned Klutak. When I glanced at my partner, he was smiling. He said that the lead in the bullets melted and the fire set off the powder. No harm was done.

During this time, there was a reindeer camp near the mouth of the Iowithla River. Two of the herders visited us in May. Since we were ready to leave camp for Dillingham, we loaned them our canoe, tent, and cooking gear. We then walked about eighteen miles to our skiff. It was stored at Lewis Point. Each of us carried twenty beaver pelts, blankets, and guns on our backs. When we approached our skiff, we found out that someone had taken the oars and oarlocks. Realizing we could not get home without oars, I cussed the unfortunate luck. There was no one else at the summer fish camp. Lewis Point was where the upriver Natives set up camp and subsisted during summer months. After calming down, I felt there must be something around that I could use.

Sailing down the Nushagak River with improvised mast, sail, and rudder.

I strolled the steep, gravel Lewis Point beach. I found a kayak paddle laying among the wet, brown grass. I figured that this could be used as a rudder. Soon, I found a long, crooked stick for a mast, to which I attached a blanket for a sail. Looking up at the sky, I noticed there was a perfect, light, northeasterly wind. Jumping into the launched skiff, we sailed straight downriver toward Dillingham and landed on the gravel beach at Kanakanak. Later, I sold the beaver pelts for a total of five hundred dollars, which was a lot of money back then. My first trapping experience was a success.

After the 1930s, for several beaver trapping seasons it was a family affair. My wife, Mary, and our two children, Florence and Ina, accompanied me by dog team. We mushed to the mouth of the

Iowithla. Here, we pitched a heavy canvas tent near the reindeer camp. One trapping season, it looked like spring breakup would be early, so I traveled back to Kanakanak to get my small skiff and kicker. I hauled this equipment back to the camp with my dog team. Later, I used the portable skiff to cross small streams when they flooded before breakup.

There was one stream, a branch of the Iowithla not too far from camp, that was too deep to wade across in hip boots. The snow suddenly melted off the tundra, which raised the water level. The current also became swift. I tied down the skiff on top of the basket sled and hauled it by dog team to the swollen stream. After placing the skiff at the edge of the stream, everything in the sled was loaded into the skiff. I threw the lead dog into the water and the rest of the six dogs followed. We quickly jumped into the skiff to cross the stream. After leaving the boat high on the bank, we retrieved our dogs. We continued by dog team to check our beaver sets. Later, after returning to the skiff, we again forced the dogs to swim across the cold, swollen currents with the empty basket sled.

When the tundra snow and ice in the small creeks are gone, the water level drops. It is easy then to cross in hip boots. We used the skiff and motor to locate beavers to shoot with our rifles, as long as there were open leads in the creeks and sloughs. This was before the main river breaks up. Some years, we were allowed to shoot beaver and other years we could only trap or use snares. As far as beaver limits—they varied from year to year. Sometimes a limit was ten or twenty beaver pelts per person.

When shooting at beavers, I sometimes missed. When a reindeer herder visitor heard about this, he told me not to get excited when I see a beaver. He said, "Be calm and take good aim!" The next day, I went out hunting and shot four beavers, one after another, without a miss. It was a lucky day. My wife and I generally obtained our beaver limit. After the trapping season was over, our entire family traveled home down the Nushagak River with a friend's large boat. It was always an enjoyable time as we arrived at Kanakanak Beach.

Another beaver season, around 1940, I planned to trap on the

Trapping

headwaters of Black Slough. Black Slough was a long stream running north across from Wood River. The beaver season was opened from April 10 to May 10. First, I hauled supplies and camping equipment with the dog team. I wanted to locate a big lake on the tundra, so that an airplane could land. Near a large lake with a wooded area behind, I pitched two tents with extra canvas for the ridge or "fly" for double protection from the rains. After the camp was established, my wife, Mary; my mother, Feodora; two sisters, Mildred and Elizabeth; and my youngest brother, Lawrence (who was twelve years old) flew to the camp in an airplane outfitted with skis.

My brother, Elmer, flew his Piper Cub airplane into our camp area. He checked some of the beaver sets while sufficient snow remained on the tundra. We also checked other beaver sets by dog team. There were many days when we checked the sets by walking.

When the trapping season was over, we had a total of seventy beaver pelts. A Belanca airplane outfitted with pontoons arrived, picked up my mother, wife, sisters, and the camping equipment. On the second trip, I, along with Lawrence, was the last one to leave by airplane. This plane carried my nine sled dogs and basket sled. We made it safely home.

Actual trapping was long, hard work. I worked up a lot of sweat shoveling tons of snow and picking through unnumbered yards of ice during those years. I mainly trapped by a slow, but steady dog team. When I found a beaver house, I manually dug a hole in the thick ice with an ice pick near the beaver's residence. In the watery hole, I set wire snares or traps under the ice, most times with bare hands.

I have trapped fur-bearing animals nearly all my life. I still trap with my second wife, Bessie, near Kanakanak. I do not use dog teams anymore. As long as there is snow, I ride my snowmachine. Dog teams are out of date; snowmachines have replaced them. Bessie likes to ride the snowmachine with me when I go riding and when I hunt ptarmigan. When I'd shot a ptarmigan, I'd walk over to pick it up by hand. When I chased a wounded ptarmigan, my wife would drive the snowmachine up to me. This saved me time walking back to the snowgo. The price of furs must be high in order to pay for gasoline.

Currently, fur prices are low. The only other reason to trap nowadays is to provide beaver meat, which we enjoy for the table.

Trapping is still important, especially when salmon fishing is poor. Trapping continues to supply employment for village residents, such as those who live in New Stuyahok or Manokotak. National animal welfare lobbies are attempting to outlaw use of steel traps. The highly publicized demonstrations in New York against use of furs is decreasing demand for furs. This lobby will continue to hurt the future of trapping.

I have trapped fur-bearing animals nearly all my life. I do not use dog teams anymore. I ride my snowmachine.

Not too long ago, the European Economic Community decided to push for a ban on pelts and fur products from countries allowing steel traps. The ban took effect on January 1, 1995, but it does give the trapping industry time to develop more humane ways of trapping and killing fur-bearing animals. I'm not sure how this will affect trapping in our area, but it's clear that selling furs at competitive prices may be a problem in the future. Over the years, I've seen prices rise and drop dramatically. Trapping should always be a way of life in Bristol Bay, as long as the main economic base in Bristol Bay is fishing and road linkages with a large city, like Anchorage, are not developed in the region.

Trapping

Some people believe that the wolf should be protected. This reminds me of one spring when I was beaver trapping about fifteen to twenty miles north of Wood River. While searching the area for beaver houses on the tundra creeks, I saw several locations where foxes had dug at reindeer remains. Near the reindeer carcass, I saw fresh wolf tracks. It was evident that a lot of reindeer—strays from the Iowithla herd—were destroyed that winter, and fairly recently too! Early in the morning, while checking the trapline, I saw three pairs of fresh wolf tracks on the new snow. These tracks came out of the Muklung timber line and then retreated into the timber. I probably would have seen the wolves, but I must have frightened them off with the gee, haw, and get up commands I muttered to my dog team. (These commands turned them to the right or left or also to encourage them to go faster.)

On the last day of the short beaver season, I retrieved all of my beaver sets. At one location, I was surprised to find a very fresh reindeer kill, evident by a bloody mess. The beautiful reindeer had just been taken down by the same wolves whose tracks I'd seen earlier. The shy wolves may have heard me coming and took off because of my noisy approach.

Chapter Seven

Hunting

In the spring, most male Natives used kayaks to hunt for seal. While living at Ekuk, I saw several kayaks drifting downriver on top of the ice flows. This required a lot of patience. The Natives would wait until a seal popped up. If the men were not hunting seal, they hunted saltwater ducks. The kayaks were fine boats. They were a speedy craft that moved along with homemade paddles. When you sat inside them, they smelled of game. The smell would disappear because you got used to it. The kayak frame was covered either with beluga skin or the skins of large seals. The kayak is usually known for its single open hole for a person in the middle, but I remember seeing two- and three-hole kayaks with two paddlers and a passenger sitting in the middle.

It was customary to hunt ducks and geese after the middle of April, when the migratory birds arrived. This was a dependable source of fresh and tasty meat. The Federal Department of Fish and Wildlife was not around to bother us. When the cannery people came up from the States, we usually quit hunting. Although some of the cannery workers wanted to hunt, we told them they couldn't hunt because the hunting season was closed.

Hunting Camp.

At Ekuk, I regularly hunted ptarmigan. The game I didn't use, I gave to people who could not hunt. One day, which was about twenty five degrees below zero, I didn't see any ptarmigan. I was puzzled,

Hunting

because there were always ptarmigan around the willow patches behind the village. While heading home, I checked a large alder patch to see if I could catch a glimpse of a bird or two. As I walked through the brush, a flock of ptarmigan suddenly flushed into the air. Surprised by their sudden appearance, I noticed long tunnels burrowed under the light crust of snow. Some birds had little roomy snow houses. Others had a small hole in the snow, just enough to crawl into.

While living in Kanakanak in the 1930s, I would go over to Grassy Island, a marshy area, about two miles offshore from Kanakanak Beach. There, I hunted waterfowl. Based on chance, I shot several varieties of ducks, Canadian geese, and even white-fronted California geese. Once, I shot a goose that turned out to be a goose no bigger than a duck. When I mentioned the small goose to my friends, I was told it probably came from the Aleutians. I was puzzled as to why the small geese were up this way. There were always many feeding ducks and geese at Grassy Island. Large flocks of honking geese flew over my house at Kanakanak in the spring. They were so numerous, they woke me up at three or four o'clock in the morning. This does not happen anymore because the birds may have a different flyway. The main reason is their numbers have decreased.

Before the river ice broke up, I enjoyed hunting at Grassy Island. One time, when I was done hunting, I anxiously oared homeward. The ice broke up earlier than I expected. A long stretch of river ice blocked travel; large, football field sized chunks of ice flowed at a quick, five knots per hour down river. Luckily the wooden skiff was small enough, and I was able to slide it across the one hundred and fifty feet of ice toward open water and managed to snake my way to Kanakanak Beach.

Each spring, families from Dillingham, Kanakanak, and Snag Point looked forward to camping at the picnic grounds, located directly across the bay from the village of Snag Point. Adults and children waded in their rubber boots through thick, green grass to gather seagull eggs. Like many, we ordered chicken eggs through the cannery from the States. These eggs were shipped in boxes full of salt each autumn. After we kept the eggs for three months, they were spoiled. The rest of the winter, we didn't have eggs to eat. Hunting for seagull eggs in the spring was a treat!

We received our coffee from Seattle in the form of coffee beans. These were ground up in a little hand-cranked grinder. The coffee was excellent, especially while spending time outdoors.

One winter, when I was a child, the smoking tobacco ran out. I saw Dad trying to smoke coffee grounds in his pipe. He made a grunt and said, "Not very good!" I don't remember what happened after that, but I remember Dad smoking a cigar. He probably got it from one of his friends.

Another winter, the store ran out of ammunition. We then had to use snares to catch ptarmigan. The snares were made with light twine. We placed a row of them in the willow patches. Thankfully, the plentiful ptarmigan were not very smart, and we always caught them. They made a fine roast. They are good fried, boiled, or even dried.

Chapter Eight

Dog Team Travel

The only transportation we had was dog teams in winter months and boats during summer. Dog team travel was very important to everyone. Good dog teams were prized. In the early 1900s, there was a dog-team trail marked by tripods from Bethel, Alaska, all the way into Bristol Bay. From Bristol Bay, it wound its way down to Kanatak, Alaska, on the east side of the Alaska Peninsula. When I traveled the trail as a fur buyer for my father, I could see the tripods in the fog or through drifting snow. They were built high and not too far apart. Cabins were built several miles apart on the trail, so that dog mushing travelers could camp overnight, feed their dogs, or have shelter during a blizzard

Dog mushers from Bethel, Togiak, Kulukuk, Dillingham, and the communities further east toward Naknek traveled the staked trail. The main reason to mush to Kanatak was to meet the mailboat. The mailboat from Seattle arrived once a month during the winter season.

I knew a fur trader at Goodnews Bay who regularly followed the tripod trail. He always had a sled loaded with fur. Over the years, tons of various furs and mail were transported over the dog-team trail to catch the scheduled mailboat. Importantly, individuals sick with cabin fever, also traveled the trail for passage to the States.

J.C. Lowes, an important fur trader from Snag Point, purchased thousands of dollars of fur at the Lowes store in Snag Point. Sometimes, Mr. Lowes hired several dog teams to transport fur to Kanatak. At Kanatak, the fur was loaded on the mailboat for sale in the states. I remembered Mr. Lowes and his wife made several special trips over the staked trail for a vacation or business journey to the Lower Forty-eight States.

Just a bit more about the staked trail. Usually beginning with the month of December, the mailman from Dillingham hauled First Class mail over the trail once a month until April. On the return mail run, he dropped off mail from the States at the small villages of Egegik, Naknek, and Koggiung. After Koggiung, he worked his way back to Snag Point and Old Dillingham.

When we lived at Ekuk, it was necessary for Dad to pick me and my sister up at Grandma Clark's home at Nushagak. Mushing, he had to travel from Ekuk on the beach to Clark's Point, then across the flats to Queen Slough. Crossing Queen Slough, he mushed northward on the Combine Flats and arrived at Nushagak village.

One Christmas holiday, we observed Dad coming in the distance. We were especially glad to see him. He said he was taking us home for Christmas, the next day. Sure enough, the following day, he bundled us up in the sled. Encouraging his dogs with a yell, we began our journey to Ekuk. The dogs left in a dead run. After a short while, the animals began to eat up the miles with a fast trot. At home in the warm living room, we were glad to talk to Mother and our baby sister, who we hadn't seen for months. After Christmas vacation was over, Dad took us back to Grandma Clark. We didn't want to go, but we had to continue our formal education at school there. We remained at Nushagak until Nushagak River was clear of ice. Then, we went home to Ekuk by boat for the summer activity.

While Dad was winter watchman at Ekuk Cannery, he installed a

Dog Team Travel

large, wooden water tank under our home. Before all the cannery water pipes were drained for the winter, he made sure he filled our water storage tank. This water lasted until freeze up. After freeze up, he would harness his dog team and carry three, thirty gallon wooden barrels in the basket sled to get drinking water. He would travel over a lagoon and pass through a creek one-and-a-half miles from our home to a spring located at the base of a hill. Here, he filled up the barrels with five-gallon buckets of spring water. The dogs were strong and did not tire easily. Dad and his dogs usually made a few round trips to fill up the tank under the house. Although the water tank held a lot of water and lasted a long time, it had to be filled repeatedly over the long winter. When we needed water upstairs, we had to hand pump it into the kitchen sink. This was the closest thing to running water back then.

The last two winters we lived at Ekuk, I was old enough to haul water with the dog team. My schooling had ended prematurely because Grandma Clark passed away. During this time, Dad made several round trips up to Nushagak and back to Ekuk when he needed something from the Mittendorf store. When Mr. Mittendorf left for the States, he hired Mr. Hall to manage the store. Eventually, Mr. Hall became owner of the store. This was at the time when families were beginning to move away from Nushagak. I knew business was becoming very poor.

When we moved to Clark's Point in 1920, my father would fill up the water barrels before the cannery water pipes were drained, just like at Ekuk. Although, the mushing trips for water became a regular chore, it was easier to haul water at Clark's than Ekuk. This was because there were no creeks to cross. There was only tundra, swamp and smooth, snow covered ponds to travel over. A well, with a shelter over it, was constructed about a mile away from our home at the base of a high, steep hill. It was easy to haul water. While I made the water-hauling trips, I hunted ptarmigan. The water trail passed many patches of willow brush, in which the ptarmigan fed.

Long trips by dog team were well planned with adequate clothing, overnight supplies, and food. While we lived at both Ekuk and Clark's

Point, Dad made a few trips by dog team to Snag Point. He mushed up the east side of Nushagak Bay for about fifteen to twenty miles, crossed Nushagak River, and turned west for several miles to cross Wood River, above present-day Dragnet Seafoods. Then, by traveling southward, he arrived at Snag Point.

In November 1929, a big flood on the Nushagak River occurred. We thought it was caused by a tidal wave. As a result of this flood, the high waters floated a scow off the ways (a platform used to store scows for the winter) at Wood River Cannery. The scow drifted across the river. At Nushagak, another fish scow floated off the ways. This one knocked down a building on the beach.

Flood tide waters floated a pile-driver scow off the ways at Creek Cannery. (Creek Cannery was located at what is now called Queen Slough above Clark's Point.) The pile-driver scow drifted toward Nushagak. It went dry at a creek below Nushagak Bluff. That is why the creek is still named Pile Driver Creek.

This same flood tide floated a power boat off its winter storage on the river bank at Nelsonville. The boat traveled a few miles up the Nushagak River on the flood tide. On ebb tide, the boat floated downriver. When it got close to Nelsonville, men went out with a skiff and kicker and towed the vessel to the Nelsonville Beach.

Luckily, the power boat was launched by the flood, possibly one of the reasons by Almighty God for the flood. A day later, I had to steer the boat to Clark's Point to pick up a sick child. The child needed emergency transportation to the hospital at Kanakanak. There were no airplanes then. The weather was mild. Most of the river ice was still piled up on the banks of the Nushagak River and Bay areas. Looking up at the banks, there were two- to three-foot-thick ice chunks scattered everywhere. After a successful trip, in which I left the child at the hospital, I mushed from Old Dillingham through Windmill Hill toward the town of Snag Point. My team and I had to wind through large, dirty, white ice chunks. These chunks of ice lay stranded everywhere on the flats between Windmill Hill and the settlement at Snag Point.

In 1950, when I was married for the second time, I kept seven sled

Dog Team Travel

dogs. They served my purpose well for many years. I used them to haul fresh water to my home at Kanakanak from the spring near Bradsford Creek. I drove the dogs to check the trap line. I hauled dry wood for our steambath.

Mushing was an important mode of transportation.

During springtime, the tundra becomes patchy with snow. The ptarmigan are spread out feeding on cranberries. Sometimes, I took along my wife and son, which was enjoyable. They sat comfortably inside the basket sled covered by blankets and canvas. When I shot a ptarmigan, I told my three-year-old son, William, to get out of the sled and get the bird. He was hesitant at first. He picked up the struggling ptarmigan and brought it to me. When we went hunting again, he was more willing to pick up the birds, and with a smile threw them in the sled. Sometimes, it was good walking, since the snow was hard packed from the night freeze.

Weather permitting, I also used my dog team to jig for smelt. I took my family about nine miles up the Wood River. I'd cut holes in the thick river ice with an ice pick. When I had two holes ready, my wife and I began to fish for smelt. We used small fish hooks. Sometimes, we caught many smelt. They provided some big meals for our table. The best smelt jigging area is further up on the Nushagak. It's too far to take my family for a day's outing. Nowadays, people fly by airplane up to Lewis Point to fish for the little fish. There the fishing is better. It is close to where the smelt lay their eggs in their reproductive cycle.

Travel by dog team was important. The dogs ate dry fish, which my wife put up each summer. The feed was stored away in the smoke house. Over the years, thousands of salmon fed the entire dog team. The dogs were like a second family. Each one had its own personality. They were enjoyable to keep and run. The team always knew when it was time to travel. They pawed at the snow, ran around in circles, and barked and howled madly. When they were harnessed, they jerked at the tow line, eager to be on their way. The older dogs were a bit wiser than the young ones. They seemed to conserve their energy for the long run.

Chapter Nine

Guiding

In the early days of the Kanakanak Hospital, the administration owned a dog team, and used it to transport a doctor to the surrounding communities for people who needed health care. The doctor preferred to travel to the villages that had a school house. One day, in the 1930s, a doctor at the Kanakanak Hospital approached me. He asked me if I would serve as a dog-team guide. He planned a trip to the village of Kulukuk and Togiak, over one hundred miles west of Kanakanak by dog team-trail. Since I needed work, I accepted his offer.

The next day, I drove my team up to the hospital. When the doctor was ready to leave, he had a surprise for me. The doctor had invited the local game warden to travel westward with us! If the Togiak people saw me mushing into the Togiak village with the game warden, I would hear about it. Since I made a promise to take the doctor to Togiak, I could not back out.

On an early morning departure from Kanakanak, the weather was good, mostly overcast, but the temperatures were mild. The two dog teams made quick progress as they trotted westward toward the mountains west of the Nushagak River. Many hours later, we arrived at a mountain pass between Manokotak and Kulukuk Bay. In this pass was a narrow creek with open water. I chopped a large number of frozen willow brush that grew along the creek bank. With the doctor and game warden's help, we piled a mound of willow brush into a narrow section of the open creek. When the brush pile was large enough, I drove the dog team across to the other side. I did this without getting wet. By this time, the doctor and game warden were tired. The day well spent, I decided to travel a bit further. I pitched a ten- by twelve-foot canvas tent to sleep in. Getting up at first light, we continued on our journey and arrived the same day at Kulukuk village. Since the doctor needed to stay longer, he secured overnight accommodations for us at the school house.

The Kulukuk school teacher's name was Abbie Morgan. She'd recently lost her husband, Ed. Abbie was a good host. The doctor in the school house examined the health of the school children and provided medicine. He also took care of village people who wanted medical attention.

The next day, we left by dog team for the village of Togiak. Togiak is located on the north east side of Togiak Bay. Later the village was moved to the west side of Togiak Bay. When I arrived Togiak, the Natives approached me. They asked me why I was guiding for the game warden. I said it was the doctor's fault, since I promised to bring him to Togiak, and he invited the game warden. Fox season was closed at the time. The Natives were trapping a few days after the fox season closed. The skins were still prime. The arrival of the game warden made a few people nervous.

Again, the doctor set up his office in the school house. He checked the school children first. Afterward, he took care of the immediate needs of the people of the village.

While the doctor was taking care of health needs, I noticed there were many people out in Togiak Bay. The Natives were fishing through the thick, snow-covered ice. I walked out on the bay. I

Guiding

discovered that the Natives were jigging for smelt. They were jigging through a small hole broken through the ice. The smelt were running heavy that day. One of the smelters asked if I wanted to try my luck. In a short time, I'd caught six large smelt. These smelt were much larger than the ones we caught on the Nushagak.

After smelting a little longer, I visited the Togiak trading post. Johnny Owens owned the small trading post, which was located slightly below the village of Togiak. After spring break up, Mr. Owens said he would sail his boat to Nushagak Bay to get supplies from the Mittendorf store at Nushagak. I'd heard earlier that during one of his resupply trips, it became very stormy. Looking for shelter from the open seas off Cape Constantine, he'd found shelter in a creek on the tip of the Cape. He remained in the creek for ten long days, so he named the creek "Ten Day Creek."

After spending a night at the Togiak school house, the doctor, game warden, and I mushed back to Kulukuk village. We knew Ed Morgan's death was a result of freezing after falling through the thin Kulukuk Bay ice. Abbie was taking her husband's death very hard. The doctor persuaded her to leave Kulukuk. He figured it wasn't right for her to remain alone after her husband's death. She insisted she must finish the school term that winter. She also said she would be okay. She remained at Kulukuk. Later that spring, she arrived at Nushagak. As soon as the ship arrived, she left the territory of Alaska. The North Star, a government boat, took her stateside.

After overnighting at Kulukuk, we departed for Kanakanak with the addition of Peter Krause and his dog team. Peter Krause was a well-known local reindeer herder. He suggested we try another pass through the foot hills between Kulukuk and Manokotak. We arrived in Kanakanak after a very long day of mushing.

That trip to Kulukuk will long live in my memory. This is because of the unusual collection of the doctor, game warden, and reindeer herder. I'm glad Abbie Morgan, the Kulukuk school teacher, wrote and published a book about her experiences at Kulukuk village. This book was published recently and is entitled, <u>Arctic School Teacher: Kulukuk, Alaska, 1931-1933</u>. Interestingly, Mrs. Morgan mentioned the doctor, game warden, and guide. The guide was none other than myself.

Chapter Ten

Road Construction

In the spring of 1931, the first road construction began from Kanakanak Hospital toward the community of Snag Point. The idea was to connect the health facility with the business community at Snag Point. The Alaska Road Commission, as it was called back then, established a camp a little way behind my home near the hospital. The road workers slept at this camp. A special heavy canvas tent was erected for construction workers to eat in. The camp had a cook who labored over a wood-burning cook stove. The stove was loaded with good-sized birch logs, cut from nearby trees.

Dad owned a Fordson tractor with caterpillar tracks, and the Alaska Road Commission rented it from him. After the fishing season was over, I went to work on the road. I began by cutting and laying corduroy brush and trees on swampy ground. I also dug ditches with a hand shovel. One time, I helped to dig a drainage ditch for the road. It was at least four feet wide and seven to eight feet deep. What misery! It was miserable to contend with those monsters called no-see-ums (gnats)! Digging down in the ditch, there was no wind to blow them away. I tried mosquito netting, but the holes in the net were too big to keep them out. I gave the mosquito net up. It seemed those nasty creatures were always in my mouth and ears.

The road construction project lasted a while. A year or two later, the Road Commission started road work from Snag Point toward Kanakanak to connect with the Kanakanak project. Again, after the fishing season, I went to work on the road project. My main work was digging ditches with a number two hand shovel. Later, I was allowed to haul gravel with the gravel truck. (The road between Dillingham and Kanakanak is now paved. This newly upgraded road was completed in the summer of 1991.)

Before 1937, I was hired to work as a foreman for the Alaska Road Commission. As foreman, I oversaw construction and maintenance of the Kanakanak/Snag Point road. During 1937, I provided substantial local input for the planning and implementation of construction of a new highway from the present-day location of the Willow Tree Cutoff to the old site of the Wood River Cannery. The Wood River Cannery was near the location currently used by Dragnet Cannery. At this time, someone from Anchorage was in charge of the overall road construction. I felt that local road construction and maintenance should be performed by local people. Feeling strongly about this matter, in March of 1937, I drafted a letter to William A. Hesse, Territorial Highway Engineer. As a result, he assured me the job as a foreman over construction and road maintenance, which I had for several years. During this time, the largest crew I oversaw was seven men, one of whom was my father-in-law, Ernest Olsen Sr. These were all local men who worked hard digging ditches and draining the swamp of water. They also performed many tasks related to highway development.

The first few years, the Kanakanak to Dillingham (Snag Point) gravel road was usable only during summer months. When the Kanakanak Territorial School closed (due to erosion), the children were transported to Dillingham by school bus. The road was then kept

Road Construction

open year-round.

The first snow blowers entering service on the highway were small, red Ford snow blowers. They kept the road clear during snowy winter months. Nowadays, the road is kept open with modern, very efficient graders and snow equipment. It has to be an extremely rare blizzard to shut down the roads entirely.

My son, Hans Nicholson, has four children; my son, William Nicholson, has five children; and my daughter, Jane Sifsof, has two boys. Those of school age catch the school bus at Kanakanak. Now, they ride comfortably to Dillingham city schools. This occurs over very safe roads constructed to Federal and State standards. The excellent highway system insures all young people can attend school and participate in extracurricular events. Good roads have insured better travel. The quality of life has substantially improved.

Kanakanak Hospital serves many people in the region. For a long time, I supported paved roads to the hospital from the city airport. This would assure that emergency patients have a smooth ride for medical care. I am glad that this road is now paved, as a result of strong, community-wide support.

Someday, I would like to see the Aleknagik road upgraded and paved. This is vital, since Aleknagik Lake is a very scenic place to visit. This way, it promotes business and tourism development. Also important for all of us who live in the relatively remote area of Dillingham, this will provide the opportunity for automobile travel outside of Dillingham. Family outings and other enjoyable outdoor events will be made possible. There are still times when the Aleknagik road is impassable, especially in spring. The thaw bubbles up through the gravel road, resulting in soft, muddy holes that will practically swallow the front end of a car.

Chapter Eleven

Taxi Service

When the gravel road between Kanakanak and Snag Point was opened up in the early thirties, I felt there was a need for a taxi service. After purchasing a Durant automobile with four doors, I began one of the first taxi services in Bristol Bay. My purpose was to provide transportation from Snag Point to Kanakanak Hospital. Transportation to the local airport was also important. Taxi service was something new to the young people. They rode back and forth several times a day. Fares were cheap. I only charged fifty cents each way, and one dollar for a round trip. A few years later, taxis began charging one dollar each way. Today, if a taxi has one passenger, it costs over eight dollars one way.

During my first years in the taxi business, Sonny Groat, a commercial air taxi pilot, used to call me by radio from Naknek. Answering from my home at Kanakanak, he informed me that he had passengers for Dillingham, Snag Point, or patients for the Kanakanak Hospital. When he flew to the villages in the region to pick up passengers, he usually radioed his wife at Naknek, who in turn relayed a message to my home. Sonny landed at the Dillingham airport. I got a lot of taxi business through him. Later, when he left from Kodiak Island on a return trip toward Naknek, his airplane crashed between the mountains and Egegik, and he was killed. I really missed him and his business after that tragic mishap.

I drove my taxi on and off until the 1960s. Once, while I was driving for profit, there was a typhoid epidemic in Bristol Bay. No one knew how it got started. It probably began from poor sanitation and drinking bad water. The sick person, or their relatives, generally chose my taxi cab to take them to the hospital. I served a lot of sick people. I had one die within two hours after reaching the hospital. After this experience, I was worried, and told the doctor I might get sick too! He said, "As long as you keep your hands clean, you probably won't get it." So I began to wash my hands with diluted Lysol and water. I even washed the car's steering wheel and door knobs with full strength Lysol. My immune system was probably very good, so happily, I didn't get sick.

Although the first ambulance in the present Dillingham area may have been a taxi, now the City of Dillingham has several very modern, well-equipped ambulances. They are used for emergencies to transport people to the Kanakanak Hospital. The City of Dillingham also has a fire station and two fire substations. The substations are located at the Lake Road and at the airport. These help immeasurably to keep home insurance premiums down. The firemen and Emergency Medical Technicians (EMTs) are all volunteers. They are well trained, and are saving lives.

Photo Album

My father, Hans P. and mother, Feodora Nicholson, in front of their home at Old Dillingham in 1935. During his life, Dad worked as a salt salmon processor, cannery watchman, postmaster, fur buyer, and magistrate. He owned the Nicholson Trading Post at Old Dillingham. Being community oriented he served on the school board.

Me, age five years, alongside my sister, Emma, age four. I didn't like the short leg pants I wore. I told my mother, I didn't like to wear them. She said I had to! And when I get older, I could wear longer leg pants. When I began wearing long pants, it made me extremely happy.

My mother and sister, Emma, in 1950. Emma was the one who financed the publishing of my book. Emma is second of ten children born to my mother. I was the eldest of the family. My father came from Copenhagen, Denmark and was a full-blood Dane. My mother, daughter of John W. Clark, was half Russian, quarter English, and quarter Aleut.

Me on a balmy calm day, summer of 1939. This is the sailboat, which I sailed for Libby's Cannery at Ekuk, Alaska. This was one of the speediest boats with which I fished commercially for salmon. Most of the Alaska Packers Cannery's boats were more beamy and as a result were slower. I enjoyed it when a brisk wind bent the mast.

above Me at the Atlas Engine Works at Oakland, California in 1924. Earlier, I left Alaska to learn a trade as a machinist. I found out during my work at the Atlas plant, that even for an expert machinist, it was difficult to find work. This is what changed my mind from learning a trade. I told myself, it would be better for me to go back to Alaska and stick with commercial salmon fishing and trapping fur-bearing animals. below Another shot of the Atlas Engine Works.

My brother, Herbert, next to Dad's 1934 Ford. Herb became a pilot, and is honored at Lake Hood's Museum in Anchorage. He was a pioneer pilot in Bristol Bay. He became a partner, with his brother, Elmer, and started the Nicholson Air Service, the first local air service out of Dillingham to Anchorage. Later, Northern Consolidated Airlines purchased the airlines. Wein Air Alaska bought out Northern Consolidated Airlines. After Wein Air went bankrupt, MarkAir took over passenger service to Anchorage.

My brother, Elmer, in front of two engine aircraft he flew in the 1950s. This picture, taken in the mid-50s, is one of many airplanes which Elmer flew. He flew his entire life, dedicating many years to flying commercially out of Bethel, Alaska. Although he had his share of accidents, I don't know of anyone who was severely injured.

above This is a sailboat half-loaded with salmon on a relatively calm day. As someone has said, these were "iron men in wooden boats." If Bristol Bay still had sailboats, we probably wouldn't have any need for limited entry. below A sailboat crew rowing to deliver a few salmon to the tally scow. This happened when there was no wind. This is a rare photograph of Alaska Packers Cannery's boat number 44. The "A" after the number 44 stands for Alaska resident fishermen. Those who came from the Lower Forty-eight States to fish Bristol Bay had boats with only a number, so it was easy to tell the difference from locals and outsiders. photo submitted by Harvey Samuelsen

above The boat's crew—a captain and one crew member. When pulling and picking fish, one man is on the corkline side, the other man is on the leadline. below A typical sailboat scene in early 1900s. Boats were dotted all around the horizon. Pacific American Fisheries' boats were painted white with black trim. Alaska Packers Cannery's boats were painted dark blue. Ekuk's boats were easy to see, since they were painted Libby yellow.

No Half Truths

Me, fueling up John Walaka's air taxi. Gas came in two, five-gallon cans to a case. John Walaka was my brother in-law. He was married to Mildred. John Walaka flew for Northern Consolidated and was a co-owner of the company.

My dad's snowmachine during the last part of the 1920s. Before any roads were constructed, it was a good vehicle to use. It was able to go through four feet of soft snow. It had caterpillar tracks with extra wheels and skis in front.

Russian Orthodox Church built in 1904 at Nushagak. When I went to school at Nushagak, and stayed at Grandma Clark's, I helped to ring the church bells during the holidays. The bells were located on the other side of the entry way.

Russian Orthodox Church at Ekuk in 1940s. Traveling priest arrived to hold service during the summer months. It was in this church that my friend, Father Bill Sifsof, officiated in the services. submitted by Mrs. Bill Sifsof

This is the first Moravian Church at Dillingham. Mildred Siebke, our first full-time missionary (middle person), served in the 1950s. Mary Carlson is on the left. The lady's name on the extreme right is unknown.

My second family at Ekuk in 1958. The tent frame is where I pitched a ten-foot by twelve-foot canvas tent for my family to live in. They lived here when I fished for salmon at Ekuk Cannery.

My son, William, near the back entrance of my home at Kanakanak. William used the three-dog team to pull a sled load of drinking water in 1967. When my house was built in 1930, I hired a carpenter from San Francisco to put up the frame and the windows. The rest of the house was finished by myself.

above My huge woodpile in 1940. This spruce and birch wood was hauled by my dog team. The logs were sawed by hand and cut with an ax. below This is a smaller woodpile in August of 1994. I split this wood with a 14 pound sledge hammer and wedge. This wood was for our steambath or maqi.

Bessie, my wife and two daughters, June; right, and April; help pull in our Kanakanak Beach subsistence net in 1975. The subsistence salmon net is used to catch king salmon. After splitting the salmon, it's flesh is installed into one-gallon tin cans. The cans are filled with water so the flesh does not get freezer burns.

My conversion running one day in 1967. These boats were not legal until 1951.

We were always drenched, since I steered in the back. This is my son, Hans, and me in 1967.

I've picked thousands of salmon in my lifetime. I had poor seasons and good ones. I remember the good fishing seasons of 1944 and 1945. Both of these years, I had about sixty thousand fish caught for Ekuk Cannery.

Flat calm day pulling in the net. If you look closely you will see that I wasn't using the hydraulic roller. The boat was low enough and calm enough so that, it was not so difficult to pull in the fish.

After pewing salmon for several decades, a new brailer method of delivery was first used by the mid-1960s. Later, when the fish-by-the pound bill was passed by the Alaska State Legislature in the early 1970s, the brailer was weighed with the fish in it.

My boat and my son, William's, skiff stored for the coming winter at Kanakanak in 1967.

above My son, William (third person from left), was President of the Bristol Bay Herring Marketing Cooperative, Inc. delegation which traveled to negotiate with Japanese companies in 1987. Here, he is negotiating with Japanese Longline Gillnet Association officials in a hotel in Tokyo. Out of this came a joint venture agreement for the Japanese to purchase herring direct from many Bristol Bay Togiak herring gillnet fishermen. Others pictured are Paul Hansen, Naknek (first left); Andrew Golia, Dillingham (second from left); Joe McGill, Dillingham (President of Alaska Herring Corporation on William's right); Ray O'Neil, Soldotna (right of Joe); and Paul Kelly, Anchorage (Attorney). below S. Takaoka (standing), President of the Japanese Longline Gillnet Association, giving a presentation to the BBHMC officials, an organization which William headed from 1979 to early 1990s. Picture was taken in 1987.

My wife, Bessie, loves to split subsistence king salmon. After splitting the fish, she hangs them on a drying rack to dry for a number of days. Then she brings them one by one into the smoke house for smoking. After smoking the strips, they are cut into short pieces, which are placed into vacuum pack plastic bags. The bags are then stored in the freezer. She does this each summer. This picture was taken in 1980.

Here, Bessie is tying strips for the smoke house in 1980. The salmon strips are delicious, especially with Eskimo ice cream in winter months.

No Half Truths

above I was proud to display several beaver pelts I trapped for in 1988. I've trapped red fox, land otter, mink, and beaver my entire life. Trappers used to make a good living. Nowadays, it is usually not possible, since other employment is necessary with a higher standard of living. below These are some of my grandchildren from my sons, William and Hans, and daughters, Jane and June. The photo was taken in 1989.

Victor Sifsof winning one of his many races. He was the first place finisher for several years at the Western Alaska Championship Sled dog races in Dillingham. These races are timed to occur during the annual Beaver Roundup festival in Dillingham. This is an enjoyable time when residents from the surrounding villages bring in their furs to sell to fur buyers.

No Half Truths

My son, William, did real well racing his dog team. Here's two of his lead dogs, Nellie, right and Chuckles, left). The dogs are a bit tired after running 22 miles in a competitive heat which lasts for three days. Running dogs was a family affair for William. We all helped him. My wife put up dried fish for feed. I repaired his sled.

This is one of the many salmon gillnets, I've hung. One night I surmised that I made enough knots (six to nine inches apart) hanging leadlines and corklines my entire life equivalent to over 300 miles of line. These knots were made to hang cork and lead lines to the web of the salmon nets.

above My friend, Bob King, who is presently the chief press secretary for Governor Tony Knowles of Alaska, presented me with the Alaska Legislature certificate that helped me to celebrate my 89th birthday. This certificate was given to me in April 1995. I thank former state representative, Mike Davis, for making this possible. below Here I am making a few remarks after receiving my Bristol Bay Senior Fishermen award from Harvey Samuelsen in 1988. Harvey, pictured on left, is president of the Western Alaska Cooperative Fishermen Marketing Association (WACMA).

Before I took up skating again, the last time I went skating was when I was twenty one years old. sixty three years went by before I began skating again at eighty four years of age. I still skate at eighty nine years of age.

My younger sisters (left to right) - Mildred, Emma, and Elizabeth. Emma funded the publishing of this book for which I am eternally grateful for. Emma's husband, Nick Raven, was a Ford and Chevrolet Car sales and garage business owner in San Francisco. Nick and Emma were also in the motel business in Mountain View, California.

My brother, Lawrence's family. Here is his wife Martha and two daughters, Kathy (left) and Sharon (right). Lawrence was a crew member onboard my sailboat. Although Lawrence did not like sailing, he later purchased a Bristol Bay limited entry salmon permit, purchased an aluminum boat, and fished quite successfully for several years before his death in 1993

My first son from my first marriage, Edward Nicholson.

My first daughter, Florence, with husband Harvey Samuelsen. Florence and Harvey have been married since the sailboat days. Harvey says, "Florence is the best fishing partner I've ever had! When, Florence had to stay home due to illness, I had to replace her with two men." They have two children, Robin and Donna.

My daughter, Ina Marsh. She lives in Anchorage, Alaska. She has three children, Dean, Ronald, and Eileen, and four grandchildren, Jerami, Christopher, Ronald Jr., and Skyler. Her husband flew for Wein Air Alaska as a jet pilot. He died in 1989.

My daughter June's family—Jay Hoover and two children, Kyle (right) and Jason (left). June works as a teller at National Bank of Alaska.

My daughter Jane's family—Victor Sifsof, Jane and two boys, VG (left) and Byron (right). Jane works for Housing Urban Development in Dillingham, Alaska. She takes time off to go commercial fishing each summer.

My son, Hans' family—Hans and Danesa with children (left to right), Robert, Mark, Jennifer, and Ryan. My son Hans started fishing with me when he was twelve years old. He has been married for twenty years now and takes his wife, Danesa, and four children fishing each summer.

My son, William's family—William and Barbara with children, Shawna (left), Parsha (Shawna's holding her), Jerilyn Bessie" (Barbara is holding her), John W. (boy closest to William), and Earl (bottom right)

My daughter April's family—Adolf "Buddy" Roehl with daughter, Erin. April is employed at Choggiung, a local village corporation, and works as bookkeeper.

Me and Bessie in front of our home at Kanakanak.

Me and Bessie in front of her much used subsistence fish and drying rack.

John W. and Bessie Nicholson, 1992

Chapter Twelve

People in the old days were very sociable. They generally knew one another well. Many regular dances were held at Clark's Point, Ekuk, Snag Point, Nushagak, Dillingham, and Kanakanak. A person planning such an event would publicize it by saying they were going to schedule a dance at a certain date at a certain place, such as in the Dillingham school house. The person, or group of people, planning the event, prepared and paid for all the food. This was provided free of charge to those attending the dance. Ham sandwiches, pies, cakes, donuts, and coffee were usually served during the last part of the dance. After the dance, someone else would announce that they were going to have a dance at the Kanakanak School House.

The Native communities had a dance hall, called qasgiq, where they danced and gave away gifts. The qasgiq served not only as a community center, but a place to build kayaks, sleds, or other woodwork, such as arts and crafts. A fireplace was located in the middle of the floor. The building had a big opening on top of the roof for the smoke to go out. When the Natives wanted to steambathe, they waited for the smoke to die down and covered the top hole. The rocks were hot by then, and water was splashed on the rocks. The steambath was enjoyable. Afterward, anyone who wanted to, washed themselves with water and soap, which always seemed available. Now, the qasgiq is a thing of the past. Nowadays most locals have their own steambaths or maqis. These are used to socialize in. They are very similar to present-day saunas.

Christmas programs were held in the schools. Christmas trees were decorated beautifully and thoughtfully. The children sang Christmas carols and acted in many interesting Christmas plays with themes lending support to the Christmas spirit. The programs were always very enjoyable. Besides Christmas plays, there were band concerts and spring plays, and programs were scheduled for anyone who was interested in attending them. All of the children, especially in elementary school, were involved in these special events. Life during the old days might not have been as intense as today, but there was a good variety of social events.

Although we were busy much of the time, because of our subsistence gathering life-style, we always had social events to attend. Work, in a sense, was as enjoyable as social events. We had to keep the home wood stoves burning to cook and heat our homes. We had to go out to the woods and chop trees down with a hand axe. Then, we loaded the heating wood on a specially made wood-carrying sled. This sled was usually pulled by nine to eleven sled dogs. The wood was hauled home and stacked on end so it wouldn't be covered by snow in the winter. Later, the stacked timber was sawed by hand. The logs were cut with a long, crosscut saw into stove-length pieces, split, and stored in a wood shed. All day long, during the cold winters, we loaded wood into the wood-burning kitchen stove. We also loaded it before going to bed. When we sleepily awoke in the morning, the house was usually cold. Sometimes I found myself shivering when I started a new fire in the kitchen stove.

Much of our work was done the hard way! We had no power chain

Social Life

saws. We didn't have the convenience of electricity. The kerosene lamps were filled each evening. We put up dried salmon to feed the sled dogs during the long, cold winter months. The dogs had to be fed each day. All this was done besides my trapping and hunting efforts. It made for a very busy life-style.

Chapter Thirteen

 # Airplanes

Airplanes were not present in Bristol Bay until the early thirties. During this time, they arrived infrequently from Anchorage. Landing fields were not available. So, in winter time, they landed on the tundra snow at Kanakanak. Since Dad ran the variety store and had room in his home, he supplied pilots with food and lodging. He also supplied their planes with gasoline. If a pilot wanted ten gallons of fuel, he received two, five-gallon cans to a case.

In summer, when the winds were calm enough, airplanes with pontoons landed in Nushagak Bay near the Kanakanak gravel beach. When the pilot decided to remain overnight, the pontoon airplane was powered up over the mud flats. They were secured by throwing an anchor and line onto the muddy bottom. Over the years, many airplanes laid at overnight rest in the little bite above Kanakanak, north of the Nelsonville (Olsonville) settlement.

During 1940, my brother, Elmer Nicholson, purchased a Piper

Cub. The Cub was a small plane on skis. Elmer learned to fly it by taking flying lessons from a local instructor. Those days, some pilots soloed after eight hours of practice. Elmer was able to solo, with the instructor's graces, in five hours of time. Currently, I understand it takes at least twenty hours of actual flying time before one is allowed to solo, depending upon the instructor.

One day, Elmer made a forced landing at Snake Lake. Snake Lake is located almost twenty miles northwest of Kanakanak. The motor suddenly quit. He managed with great skill to land the Cub. The aircraft came to rest about fifty-five feet from the shoreline. As soon as the plane stopped, the skis broke through patchy snow and ice. After looking things over, Elmer realized that the skis were in about two-and-a-half feet of water. There was no damage to the Cub. Knowing that the ice was pretty thin in the cold, outdoor temperature, Elmer rolled himself to more secure footing inshore. If he stood up on the ice, he probably would have broken through. Elmer also knew that wet feet were dangerous when the temperatures were extreme.

The temperature dropped to minus eighteen degrees as Elmer walked. He walked in a southeasterly direction from the west side of Snake Lake. After some difficulty moving through a thick willow brush patch, he arrived at a small trappers cabin. The cabin was located about two miles from the lower end of Snake Lake. At the cabin, a man with a dog team offered to carry him to Kanakanak.

When Elmer arrived home, he immediately sought me, his older brother. He asked me to help him retrieve his plane. Although I was tired from my day's work, I rounded up some rope and hitched up the dog team. Both of us traveled through the darkness to the cabin at Snake Lake. At the cabin, we slept until daybreak.

After coffee, we left for the downed airplane. Once there, noticing that the ice was thick enough to walk on, I began to chop ice to make a path for the aircraft skis toward shore. After this was done, I tied a doubled rope to the prop. I ran the line back to a strong brush on shore. I then put a heavy stick between the two ropes. With the stick, I began spinning the rope. By spinning the rope, it shortened the line. In this fashion, I was able to move the plane closer to shore. After repeating

Airplanes

this several times, the Cub was successfully pulled on top of the lake ice near the willows.

Elmer quickly installed an engine cover over the motor. He fired up the pot burner to heat the engine. Later, after some hot coffee, boiled on my camp stove, he entered the Cub, seated himself, and primed the motor. After hitting the switch, the engine started. The motor appeared to run fine. He didn't know why the engine quit earlier, but he taxied out anyhow. I was surprised when Elmer throttled the plane for takeoff. I saw the Cub gather speed, bounce, and go airborne. As I peered at the sky under cotton gloves, Elmer's Cub was soon a small speck on the horizon, headed for home.

I hurriedly prepared the dog team for departure. I found out later that it took Elmer fifteen minutes to fly home, where he tied down the Cub in front of Dad's place. It took me over three hours to mush through timber, creeks, and open tundra to Kanakanak.

During World War Two, an army DC-3 type airplane made a forced landing in the tundra swamp near Snag Point Hill. Since the aircraft sustained little damage, a crew of army personnel flew to Dillingham to see if they could retrieve what they thought was a flyable airplane. They got local heavy equipment to grade the hill, and create a small airport. They pulled the downed aircraft onto the newly constructed airfield, patched it up, and took off. With a little more improvements, this small airfield became Snag Point's first new airport.

Soon, some of the local pilots who had pontoons and skis outfitted their airplanes with wheels. They began to operate out of the new airport. This occurred because the airport was close to Dillingham's business center. Dependence upon the Lily Pond and Nushagak Bay for pontoon landings was lessened with an airfield. The airfield provided landings in virtually any kind of moderate wind conditions, however, it was too short to land the larger airfreight transports.

Small, air taxi bush planes with pontoons continued to fly to Dillingham. Pontoon landings enabled them to land close to Kanakanak Hospital. Weather permitting, they landed close to Dillingham or Kanakanak Beach. If the water was too choppy, they landed in

103

Shannon's Lake near the Aleknagik Road or the Lily Pond near town.

Years later, Dillingham received enough funds to construct and operate a modern, longer airport. This airport is presently located due north of Squaw Creek and west of New Dillingham by at least two miles. The airport terminal was originally on the east side of the gravel airport. Later the buildings were moved to the west side, where more expansion was possible. This expansion area accommodated new air-taxi services, airfreight airlines, repair facilities, and tie-down space. In the 1980s, the airport was topped with an asphalt base, which was a tremendous improvement. This eliminated the dust problem created by a gravel runway. Presently, Alaska Airlines 737 jet airplanes land several times daily on scheduled passenger and cargo runs. Passengers are quickly flown to Anchorage within a mere hour.

Today, there are a lot of small, privately owned airplanes parked near the asphalted air field. With newly expanded parking areas, there is plenty of room for planes to be tied down securely, with protection from strong winds. My sons, Hans Nicholson, William Nicholson, and my son-in-law, Victor Sifsof, have their airplanes parked here.

As in the past, with my brothers Elmer and Herbert, aircraft served a purpose. They both spent most of their lives in the air as air-taxi pilots. Airplanes continue to have great importance as a primary means of transportation to people living in the area.

Today's airplanes have an added purpose besides transportation. Victor Sifsof uses his Cessna 170B airplane to spot herring at Togiak for his seine boats. He has a power scow that pumps the herring out of their seines. The scow delivers the herring to the processor. After the Togiak herring season, his scow picks up salmon from power boats for a local fish buyer. His airplane is of vital importance for supportive work, and he flies for parts and equipment to keep his fishing operation going.

Chapter Fourteen

Alaska Territorial Guard

During World War One, I was too young for the draft. I knew some salmon cannery workers who said that when they returned to the States, they'd be drafted. President Wilson asked Congress to declare war on April 2, 1917. Congress voted on April 6, 1917, to declare war. Germany was sinking our ships in the Atlantic Ocean.

When the United States entered the big war, the name "hamburger" was dropped in Bristol Bay, due to its German origins. Hamburger steaks were called liberty steaks, or some other name other than hamburger. We also had a problem of getting real flour during the war. I remember my father saying, "Imitation flour, again!" There was no pure, white flour available for a period of time. Although I was just eleven years old, I knew there were other food items we could not order from Seattle.

During 1924-1925, I was in San Francisco. I heard rumors that, eventually, we were going to have a war with Japan. I heard this

105

seventeen years before it actually happened. While in San Francisco, I saw, firsthand, several large Japanese battleships anchored out on the bay. Some of the Japanese sailors came ashore. I saw them walking up and down Market Street. At the time, I didn't believe the rumors of eventual war with Japan.

The same year, I also saw American war ships in San Francisco Bay. Since the public was invited out to board the ships, I decided to visit one. I managed to board a small launch to tour one of the ships. On board the battleship, a guide took us through the ship. I saw large gun barrels sticking out of the heavily armored turret. I wanted to go inside the gun turret, but the guide informed me this was off limits.

The fall of 1924, employment was becoming difficult to find in California. I was lucky to obtain an apprentice job in a machine shop in Oakland, California. I became acquainted with a machinist who worked there. My machinist friend told me that, earlier, an expert machinist came to the shop seeking employment and was turned down. A man with skills found it difficult to locate work. Later, in the early thirties, things were even more terrible. They named it the Great Depression. There were soup lines stretched out for blocks in cities in the Lower Forty-eight States. In Bristol Bay, the depression did not affect us. Life went on normally. Nowadays, if the South Forty-eight, enters a recession period, it affects us. It results in higher prices for commodities and lower fish prices, which ultimately effects our quality of living.

World War Two started when Japan bombed Pearl Harbor in Hawaii on December 7, 1941. Soon, all the young men in our area were required to register for the draft. I also registered.

Feeling I might be drafted anytime, I went out into the woods to cut trees for firewood in consideration for my family. My intention was to cut enough firewood to last for at least three winters. When I was done, my friends said, "What a big pile of firewood!" I also had two taxis at the time of the "day of infamy."

Later, I knew I wouldn't be able to buy new tires. They were impossible to get, so I sold the two cars before the tires wore out. Although we had plenty of flour, there was no Budweiser beer to be

Alaska Territorial Guard

purchased anywhere in Dillingham. I always wondered if the Army got it all.

An Army Signal Corps station was established at Kanakanak before World War Two. When the United States declared war on Japan, the station personnel hired three civilian guards for eight-hour shifts. I was employed as one of the guards. I used my trusty, old 30.30 Winchester rifle for guard duty.

When war broke out, the people in our town were ordered to cover their windows at night. It was dark at night. One of my local neighbors tried to scare me by sneaking up on me during guard duty at the signal station.

An Army official arrived in Dillingham to recruit men for the Alaska Territorial Guard. I joined the Territorial Guard. Although we were members of the Guard, we were allowed to continue commercial fishing during summer months and trapping fur-bearing animals during winter.

Initially, we drilled with broomsticks for rifles. Later, we were issued old, used World War One Springfield 30.06 caliber rifles. The ammunition issued was no good. The ammo leaded up the Springfield's bores. The members of the local Guard unit were prepared to go to war at any moment. Some members of the local Guard unit were transferred into the regular Army. Some of them served in the Aleutians and experienced actual combat. For me, I guess, I was too old. Orders never arrived for service. What was also good—the Japanese did not arrive. I didn't have to harm any of them. When I left the Guard unit, I was a sergeant.

Over twenty years later, I was awarded a State of Alaska certificate for service in the Alaska Territorial Guard from 1942-1947. I am proud of this award, which hangs prominently on a wall in my living room.

Chapter Fifteen

Reindeer Herding

In 1920, I dickered with Peter Krause, who owned a herd of reindeer at Kulukak. For twenty-five dollars a head, I purchased ten female and two male reindeer. In the bargain, Peter agreed to keep them in his herd for six years. Finally, during the winter of 1927, Peter drove my reindeer from Kulukuk to Old Dillingham.

During the six years, my reindeer mated and grew in number. When Peter was bringing my animals to Dillingham, I really didn't know how many I owned. I was waiting for the herd. When I saw them at last, moving through the low hills slightly west of Nelsonville, I was surprised as to how large the herd was. I saw a sea of moving horns and tan-and-white-colored fur moving on the open tundra. There were adult animals, as well as young ones. They were indeed beautiful animals.

As my reindeer arrived into a spruce tree area, they noticed a bunch of reindeer that belonged to a man named Nelson (these reindeer were waiting to be butchered). My entire reindeer herd quickly galloped in a beeline for the security of Nelson's herd. As they entered the herd, I hurriedly counted them. I tallied seventy-seven head. Later, I arranged to keep my reindeer with Nelson's herd. It was easy to keep them separated, since the ones I owned had their own distinct ear-markings.

Needing someone to look after my growing herd of reindeer, I asked John Evan, a boy from the Dillingham Orphanage, if he'd like to earn some money. He agreed to care for my reindeer. It was important for him to look after the newborns. Once he discovered a newborn, it must be immediately earmarked. The ear-marking established ownership. Another job was to castrate males. Once castrated, they were later butchered. Castration is important, so that the flesh would develop more fat. With more fat, the reindeer meat was tastier.

In order to care for my reindeer herd, I constructed a reindeer sled for John Evan. This sled was built low. It was a little wider than a basket sled, which was generally used for mushing. I built this sled, so John could train reindeer to pull the sled. Since the herd is constantly moving from one place to another, it helped John to relocate with the herd. Movement of the herd was vital, so tundra feeding areas were not overgrazed.

By 1929, my herder said I had 109 reindeer. The numbers continued to grow. Nelson and I shared a trained reindeer dog. In turn, John and Nelson used the dog to keep their reindeer together. With the dog, it was easier to control the herd. Since the reindeer were nearby, it supplied our families with fresh meat for several years.

Eventually, reindeer herding became threatened. Commercial salmon prices began to rise. Some of the local herders began to fish. They left the reindeer herds. This impacted the reindeer economy severely. When fishing season arrived, no one was around to take care of the hundreds of reindeer.

When fishing season was over, and if an airplane happened to be in Dillingham from Anchorage, the pilot was hired by the more affluent to look for the reindeer. By this time, they were scattered all

Reindeer Herding

over the tundra. Since these were scattered, only a few bunches were located. After the reindeer were located, the herders traveled by foot to round them up. Many strays were not found. This occurred year after year, until there was a significant reduction in the Dillingham and Nushagak River area reindeer herd. These strays gradually moved further away into caribou country up the Nushagak River. They mixed in with the wild caribou.

About this time, I heard a reindeer report. The report stated that the reindeer had overgrazed the country. The report also said that they might eventually become extinct. I agreed that it probably was happening further north in Alaska. I disagreed with it for our area. There was, and still is, virgin country reindeer never set foot on.

During the heyday of reindeer herding in the 1930s, a trader from Goodnews Bay operated a cold-storage facility. This facility was located about a mile west of the present-day Dragnet Fisheries processing plant near Wood River. When the cold storage was first built, everyone in town was invited for a special dance celebration. That night, I saw about sixty or so people who attended the dance. The room was packed full of characters. As, usual there was plenty of food and drink. The building had a small door for an entry. It had no windows for light. While we were dancing, the oil lamps became dimmer and dimmer. Someone said to me that the oxygen was being used up. Someone finally thought to open the door. By that time many of the dancers began to leave and the dance soon ended.

Lapps from the Kuskokwim River area sold a large herd of reindeer to the trader at Wood River. As part of the deal, two Lapps drove the entire herd from the Kuskokwim to the Snag Point area cold storage. They were quickly slaughtered and butchered. After butchering, the meat was frozen by a gasoline-run freezer generator. The meat was available for a limited market.

The salmon packing canneries did not bring fresh meat up from the States to feed their workers. As a sailboat fisherman, I had the opportunity to eat at the cannery cook house. The menu had fresh, Outside meat only during the Fourth of July. The Chinese cooks slaughtered and butchered a live pig. This was a delicacy. The cannery also kept live chickens. These were nurtured, killed, and cooked for the Blue Room table, a special room where the superintendent, cannery foreman, machinist, bookkeepers, and others ate their dinner.

Reindeer was a major source of locally produced meat. The trader at Wood River ran his power boat to deliver frozen reindeer meat on demand to each cannery on Nushagak Bay. Once the cannery cook received the reindeer meat, the shipment was placed in a small, cold-storage locker, next to the cook house.

When the steamer ships from Seattle replaced the sailing freighters, they had refrigeration. As a result, the salmon packing companies brought their own meat supplies. When this occurred, the trader's reindeer meat business at Wood River closed down.

Chapter Sixteen

Commercial Salmon Fishing

I fished salmon commercially for the first time when I was eleven years old. As a teenager, I setnetted on Ekuk's sloped gravel beach from 1917 to 1920. Moving to Clark's Point the next season, I continued to setnet not far from the pile-driven cannery docks. That same season, I switched to driftnetting, which was more efficient. I began to catch fish with a double-ender sailboat in 1921, and fished until 1925. From 1926 to 1938, I fished successfully for Wood River and Clark's Point Canneries. I agreed to fish for Ekuk Cannery in 1939. Similar to most fishermen, I preferred to drift with a sailboat. The canneries provided boats and gear.

One day, when I was still setnetting, I glanced out at Nushagak Bay from the beach at Clark's Point. On a flat calm day, several sailboats were drifting up the bay off Ekuk Church, which is nestled against the Ekuk Bluff. Fishing was slow. Swirling, dark smoke emulated from the open boats. The black smoke was produced from burners, a cook stove that fishermen used. These burners were an upright cylinder stove fueled by wood or coal. Brewing a pot of coffee or warming up food in tin cans took the chill and hunger away. Later, the invention of the Swede Stove was a blessing for fishermen. It eliminated the smoke, which was a bother.

The Swede Stove had a container below the burner, which was filled with kerosene. A hand air pump attached to the side provided air that forced fuel to the burner. When we fished, we poured a little alcohol on the burner to light the burner. When the flame was almost burned out, the kerosene valve was opened. The flame put out a lot of heat; hot coffee was made in no time. In order to shut the burner off, we simply shut off the flow of kerosene.

The alcohol to prime the Swede Stove was used for another purpose. After fishermen laid out their nets to fish for a longer period of time such as during a night set, they took the mast down. Once the mast was down, they pitched a tent on the bow of the boat. Their bedding was kept under the bow, which was covered with a heavy, waterproof canvas. Before the bedding was rolled out, the floor was usually damp or wet. A bit of alcohol was poured on the wooden floor boards. A match was set to it, and the flame dried the floor out.

During the sailboat era, fishermen laid out their gillnets and went to sleep during the night. They did this with little worry about drifting toward other boats. All the boats were the same size, but with different colors, based on the cannery they fished for. With the arrival of power, the boats changed in size and speed. Cabins were added. Most of the boats were wind catchers, some drifting faster, some slower. As a result, someone had to always be on watch, so the driftnet wouldn't tangle up with other nets.

Nowadays, the power boats have a crew of three to five people. Before power boats, company-owned sailboats usually had two grown men to a boat. They were called either the captain or the boat puller. While fishing, the boat puller rowed the boat, while the captain laid out the gillnet from the stern of the boat. Both men pulled the loaded nets in by hand rollers; one pulling on the cork line and the other on the lead line. There were no power rollers during the sailing days, so it was hard work. It was especially difficult during windy

Commercial Salmon Fishing

weather.

The sailboats were towed out to the fishing grounds by a gasoline-powered vessel called the monkey boat. Towing was done usually before a salmon opening. One monkey boat towed ten to twenty boats in a line from the cannery dock out to the fishing grounds. After a salmon opening, if the sailboat had no fish, the monkey boat (by company policy) couldn't tow them around. If they have fish and need to deliver to the tally scow, the monkey boat was available.

Either by sail, or towed by the monkey boat, the fishermen skillfully maneuvered their boats alongside the flat scow. This scow, tied to the tally scow (which housed the tally man and cook), was usually anchored in a protected area. The flat scow was where the fishermen pew their catch by hand, one by one. The tally man counted the fish. The fishermen were required to deliver their fish fresh, within twenty-four hours.

What was enjoyable, after pewing thousands of salmon from a good load, the fishermen ate a hardy meal. The meal was free and prepared by the tally-scow cook. After chow, the fishermen went back out fishing.

Safety was not a big concern in the early days. I fished for nearly forty seasons in a sailboat. During this period, I didn't have a life preserver or compass in the boat. The canneries had no life preservers or compasses in stock, so they were not available.

One day, before the first sailboats were launched, I saw the net boss drilling holes under the bow and stern of a boat. When I asked him what he was doing, he said that he was going to run a line circling the bottom of the boat. If the boat capsized, the fishermen would have something to hang onto. This was done during the last sailboat season before motorized boats were legal.

During the fishing season of 1918, eighteen fishermen drowned at Snake River Flats, directly across from Clark's Point. This was due to unusually rough weather, overloaded boats, and nothing to hang onto. If someone had installed the ropes on the sailboat hulls before the accident near Snake River, it could have saved many lives. It didn't seem that life was valued then, as much as it is now. Now, in the Bristol Bay fisheries, there are increasingly more vessel safety rulings coming from the Coast Guard.

Not having a compass didn't bother me. During foggy, wet, and windy weather, I always knew what stage the tide was in. For high or low water, I dropped a lead weight with a string attached over the side of the boat to find out which way the current was running. Generally, I knew from seasons of dead reckoning experience in what section of the bay I was located.

The sailboat had a center board with a steel rod to push it down. The center board kept the boat from sliding sideways when under sail. When the boat went into shallow water, the center board was forced up, which is normal. When that happened, the boat was steered to deeper water (the center board made a good fathom meter in shallow water).

Motorized fishing boats were allowed by the United States Bureau of Fisheries in 1951. Most fishermen wanted gasoline-powered vessels. I was reluctant to make the change. The first power boats were called conversions. When I heard a "hot" report of sockeye running over at Coffee Point, as long as the wind was blowing favorably, I sailed over quicker than the converted boats.

It was a thrill to see the full sail, especially when the mast bent slightly. I felt I was going like the wind. Inevitably, power won out. I finally agreed to operate a sailboat conversion the summer of 1953. Overcoming my initial hesitancy with the new vessel, I fished both the Kvichak and Nushagak Bays.

I driftnetted for Ekuk Cannery until 1959. I hung nets in the spring and fished for Pacific American Fisheries (PAF) in Dillingham. At this time, I owned a conversion I purchased from Ekuk. In the late 1970s, still with the same boat, I quit fishing after sixty-four years in the commercial fishing business. I would have fished longer, but my boat became unsafe. I was afraid the stern might fall off.

As a fishermen for Ekuk Cannery, I hung salmon gillnets for their fishermen for twenty seasons. I did this in the spring, before the fishing season opened. At PAF Cannery, I hung and mended nets for twenty years. "Old fishermen never die, they just fade away," I've

Commercial Salmon Fishing

heard said, even after retirement from the commercial fishing industry. In 1995, I continue to hang herring and salmon gillnets for my sons.

In the late 1800s, according to my father, sailboat fishermen received a set salary. Later in the development of the salmon fishery, the canneries paid fishermen two cents for a whole salmon. When I started to fish as a young man, I got five cents a fish. As I said earlier, the sailboats were company owned. The nets and the food were furnished free. Payment by the pound didn't occur until the 1970s. Nowadays, fishermen sometimes receive over a dollar a pound for sockeye. In 1993, sockeye dipped to a low of sixty cents a pound, which doesn't make sense on the open market in Japan, because the consumer is still paying the same price at the counter.

Before we'd start fishing for the season, I'd go to work on salary in early April for Ekuk Cannery. First, we'd fire up an oil-burning stove in the main bunkhouse. When the building was warm enough, we'd paint inside. We painted several bunkhouses, which took nearly a month. As the weather warmed up the first of May, we began painting fish scows, monkey boats, and tug boats. One time, there were a lot of cracked water pipes that weren't properly drained in time before freeze up, so I had to cut out the cracked sections and replace one-inch up to two-inch diameter galvanized pipe. I continued working for wages until the cannery ship arrived, then I began to work for run money.

Run money was earned through work at the cannery performed by the fishermen just before salmon fishing began. This work prepared the cannery for canning fish, and since a huge run of salmon was expected, it took much preparation. Run money was also earned right after fishing was done. Everyone made a set fee of one hundred dollars before fishing and one hundred dollars after fishing was finished.

While working on the sailing ship, we called the people on the ship, the ship gang. The ship gang unloaded the freight from scows, which was loaded by the shore gang. The net gang worked in the net house. They hung and mended gillnets.

After the fishing season was over and the ships were loaded, almost everyone returned to the States. Since I lived locally, I continued to work into the autumn. Along with four or five other men, I cleaned the inside and outside of fifty-plus sailboats owned by the cannery. After cleaning the boats, we painted them inside and out. Numbers had to be repainted on both sides of the bow and stern. After finishing work on the boats, the water pipes were drained at the cook house and all the bunkhouses. There was a lot of other work to do before the cold temperatures set in.

One year, it was a good fishing season. The fall workers quit early. With their earnings, they purchased trapping supplies and went back upriver. This left the winter watchman and myself to do all the cannery storage-related work. The work schedule and projects fell behind. Then, it got real cold! The cargo slip had to be taken in quickly. We grimly tore up the deck planking with crow bars. We needed to take the ten by twelve inch timbers into shelter. When we did this, the timbers were iced up on all sides. Surprisingly, they were easy to slide up by block and tackle for storage . After this was done, there was more painting to be done inside several heated bunk houses. That fall, mostly alone, I worked until the middle of November.

The cannery had many large, cumbersome, cast-iron machines. Coal was used to provide steam to run the cannery processing machinery. When a scow load of black, chunky coal came to shore, it was loaded with hand shovels onto wheelbarrows (this had one wheel in front and two handle bars). These wheelbarrows were lifted by the handles and pushed up on a slanting cargo slip. Once over the slip, the coal was unloaded at the coal bin behind the boiler room. It was backbreaking, sweaty, dirty work. Jitneys and wagons to tow were not available, until years later.

Ekuk Cannery installed a specially designed machine called the Iron Chink. It was a revolutionary tool, which brought salmon processing into the modern age. It efficiently cut the salmon heads off and opened the belly for sliming. After the Iron Chink did its work, the fish carcass was put on a conveyer belt. The belt carried it over to several lines of canning machines. There, the machines cut the

Commercial Salmon Fishing

salmon into pieces for the tin can. Still another mechanical device placed the flesh into metal pound cans. The filled can individually rode its course, had a lid installed, then slid into an iron rack. The rack held several dozen cans. The rack was wheeled by hand over to a steam retort. The retort cooked the canned salmon. When the salmon cans were cooked, the racks were taken out and stored in warehouses to cool off. Finally, when the cans were cooled off, they were stockpiled, can over can, to a height of about five or six feet.

When I was a child, the Chinese boss hired several kids to take the one-pound salmon cans out of the coolers and stack them. He enticed them with a few nickels and dimes. After the cans were cooled, they were placed one-by-one into wooden boxes. They had no machines then to put the cans in boxes. It was done manually. Now the shore-based canneries have machines that speed up the process. They are capable of rapidly installing tin cans in paper boxes.

After salmon fishing was over and all salmon had been canned, the fishermen loaded the wooden cases onto the scows for shipment. Salmon cases were first loaded on a two-wheeled hand truck and pushed down an incline to the scow. After the cannery purchased four-wheeled motorcars and wagons, the work became much easier. When the fishing season ended and the company quit canning, there was always a rush to get the salmon pack on board the ship. At each cannery in the bay, the fishermen elected a delegate. The delegate advised the fishermen not only where to go, but what to do to speed up the work.

Most fishermen didn't like to work aboard the anchored freighter. On the freighter, they stacked individual forty-eight-pound cases of boxed salmon deep into the ship's hold.

One day, the delegate asked me to work in the ship's hold. The same day, I became a ship's gang member. From the ship's deck, I climbed down an iron ladder that disappeared into the dark depths. It was intimidating going down this ladder. Inside the dimly lit bowels of the freighter, we toiled long hours working for a few dollars. It took from five to seven days to put the entire cannery salmon pack on board the ship. Everything was done by hand.

119

Before the cases were stacked in the hold of the ship, they first had to be handled by hand ashore and stacked on scows. At least onshore, the beach gang were able to see the sunlight or what was going on around them. Sometimes, we only got four or five hours of sleep on board the ship. The saying was, "The scow load of salmon cases must be unloaded according to the tides," so we rushed, so the scow could be reloaded by the next high tide.

Canneries didn't have electricity. A night watchman ambled around the cannery premises with a handheld kerosene lantern. They punched clocks, probably because of insurance. The cook house had a full-time baker who made bread, pies, and cakes during the night. He also used a round-burner kerosene lamp. The stove was fired with coal.

As I stated earlier, power boats were legalized to fish in Bristol Bay in 1951. Before legalization, the superintendent at Ekuk Cannery opposed power boats. The reason I was against power boats was because every Tom, Dick, and Harry might fish. Too many fishermen would fish upon a limited stock of fish. After legalization of power boats, and the establishment of limited entry in 1972, it seems there are now twice as many fishermen. These include doctors, lawyers, and other professionals; it seemed all the pencil pushers started fishing after limited entry! During sailboat days, they wouldn't have been able to fish, because they might have been afraid to sail. The rigors of sailing and living in an open boat would have been overwhelming. I may be old fashioned, but I still feel that it's only those guys that know how to harness the wind really know how to fish!

The original sailboat conversions were miserable! The engine invariably quit. The fuel line filled with water. Other troubles resulted. We kept a pair of long, wooden oars in case of engine failure. At least, we could always go by manual power.

After fishermen began fishing with conversions, the monkey boats were unnecessary. Power boats soon delivered directly to the large, wooden, power scows. One of the first scows was the Mink. The scow had a cabin on the stern. Instead of pewing the salmon up from a pitching boat into flat scows, they were pewed into brailer

Commercial Salmon Fishing

baskets that were lowered into the fishermen's vessel. The tally man used a little handheld mechanical counter. He punched it with his thumb whenever a fish was pewed into the basket.

The power scows had booms with winches protruding from the pilot cabin. These lifted the salmon-filled baskets out of the boats onto the scow's deck. During the 1970s, salmon were weighed by automatic scales installed on the brailer line. Later, fishermen installed nylon mesh brailers in their boat holds. After picking, the fish were tossed into the brailered fish hold. The brailer was simply lifted out one by one at delivery. This eliminated the need to pew fish into brailer baskets. This method was more efficient. It allowed the fishermen to return to drifting quicker, which made them more competitive. Fishermen's mentality began to change slowly. As they became competitive, especially with more comfortable, faster vessels, more fishermen went independent. More fishermen bought their own vessels after fish prices rose. Fishermen made even more money when they finally got paid by the pound, rather than by the fish.

After 1953, I was given a life preserver and a compass for the first time. Later, in the sixties, we installed two-way radios in our boats. This brought the fishermen closer together. The newer VHF radios in the seventies produced a breed of fishermen who began to work the fishery together. Groups of fishermen with radios produced more fish. Friends shared information about where schools of salmon were located. At this time, Dillingham was fortunate to receive funding for a radio station. The radio station, call sign KDLG, provided weather reports for fishermen. Also, of great convenience, the Alaska Department of Fish and Game began to announce commercial salmon opening on KDLG radio.

Before radios, we were all individualists. I kept track of where the highliner sailboats sailed. When I noticed several boats moving in one direction and a few dropping their sails in a hurry, I knew there must be a lot of fish there. I sailed to that location and sure enough, salmon were jumping. With excitement, I laid out my gillnet. Soon, I got my load of fish! I was a highliner for Ekuk one year. I knew how to locate fish myself. When a bunch of boats were fishing an area, and if there were no fish where I was, I would beat it over there. I got every bit of speed I could from the wind. I prized the Ekuk sailboat. It was a little narrower than the Clark's Point boats. It sailed faster, so with a mouth full of Copenhagen snuff and a silly grin, I spit over the side as I passed slower boats.

When the run of salmon comes into the bay on flood tide, the bulk of the fish follow the rip tide. On one side of the rip tide, a fish boat can catch a boat load of fish in a short time, while on the other side of the rip, the fisherman only gets a few. After high water, the fish sound, or disburse. In spite of much gear in the water, thousands of salmon on their perennial cycle swim upriver through the large fishing fleet toward the spawning grounds in the Wood River Lake system.

During my lifetime, we experienced poor fishing seasons. We also had good ones. The poor seasons were probably due in part to a large number of predators. One such predator was the Dolly Varden trout. In the last part of the thirties to the first part of the forties, the United States Bureau of Fisheries wanted to thin them out. The lake fishermen were paid a set salary of two-and-one-half cents for each Dolly Varden tail. Later, it was raised to five cents a tail. One fall, my father-in-law fished for Dolly Varden, which brought five cents a tail. At the headwaters of Lake Aleknagik, he made fifteen hundred dollars in a short time. There were other fishermen who made considerable money fishing for Dolly Varden in the upper Wood River lakes.

The last year of the Dolly Varden bounty, I fished Aleknagik Lake. During the sunny day, my partner and I didn't see any Dollies near shore in the crystal clear water. Fishing was poor. Soon, at dusk, I saw a wave of them coming in close. With that happy occurrence, we laid out one end of the seine on the beach. The rest of the seine was pushed out of the stern. After oaring out a distance, we rowed back hard to shore in a circular fashion. Our net was loaded with lively Dollies. The Dolly Varden bounty was established before statehood and provided a source of income for local people. After statehood, I told the Commissioner of the Alaska Department of Fish and Game that predator fishing in the Wood River Lakes built up the 1944 and 1945 salmon runs in the Nushagak Bay area. He responded that he

Commercial Salmon Fishing

didn't think so! Again, I told him flatly that all the old timers in our area felt that fishing for the Dolly Varden predators did a lot of good for the Nushagak fishery.

Other salmon predators were identified before statehood. The United States Bureau of Fisheries felt the arctic tern was eating salmon fingerlings. They also ate up a lot of salmon spawn. As a result, the United States Bureau of Fisheries sent out patrol boats. Men with shotguns blasted away at any tern they could find. For several years, this continued all summer long. Another identified predator was the hair seals swimming in Nushagak Bay. For a time, there was a cash bounty on seals. The beluga whale was also a potential predator on salmon stocks. It is locally known that this mammal can swallow several salmon in a short while. I was told by a biologist that it doesn't take long for a salmon to be digested. At the PAF dock in Dillingham, a dead beluga was hoisted onto the deck. The stomach was opened. Inside was a large king salmon. Since the throat was small, it must stretch a bit in order to swallow the king. The Nushagak king salmon is a species weighing sometimes over forty pounds. Also, when I was a young adult, during a spring seagull egg hunt at Grassy Island, I noticed smelt laying near a seagull nest. Out on a sandbar nearby, I saw hundreds of seagulls. Some of them were diving. They were feeding on small fish. I wondered if they also eat salmon smolt. It is illegal to shoot them.

No Half Truths

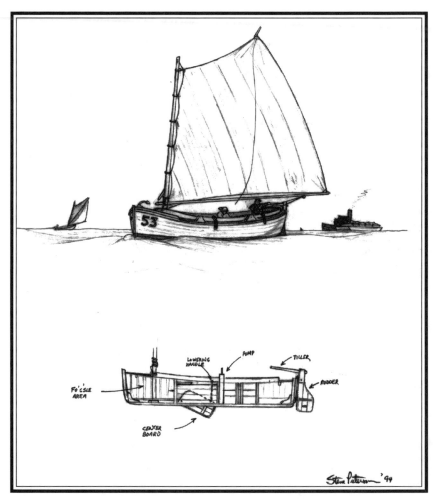

Typical Bristol Bay sailboat.

Chapter Seventeen

More Sailboat And Other Fishing Stories

At Ekuk Cannery in 1939, I decided to fish with my father-in-law, Ernest Olson Sr. A surprise awaited for me. Earlier, the superintendent had placed the boat in his name. Ernest was the captain, while I was the boat puller. That was the first and only time in my life I was a crew man. Although Ernest was a good sailor, he knew a mistake was made. He prudently allowed me to do most of the sailing throughout the fishing season. After this mishap, each spring, I made sure that a company-owned sailboat was designated in my name.

As Captain, I chose whoever I wanted as boat puller. I was careful in selecting this person. This crewman had to be strong and in good health. He not only oared the boat, but was responsible to pull the stock anchor. He also hoisted the canvas sail whenever I wanted to travel across the bay. Very important, of course, as it is today, this man should be a fast fish picker.

My father-in-law fished for Ekuk Cannery for several years. He

125

told me in that 1938, the cannery pack for the fishing season was one hundred and forty thousand cases. Since the run was large and the catch great, the cannery ran out of tin cans. The cannery superintendent had to get more cans from the Kvichak area from Libby, McNeill and Libby. The warehouses were stacked full of canned salmon cases. Because of the huge pack, Ekuk also had high piles of salmon cases stored alongside the warehouses. They were covered with heavy, scow canvas tarps.

Over the years, hundreds of sailboats fished Bristol Bay. The sailboats' numbers were painted on both sides of the bow and stern. In Nushagak Bay, we usually didn't have the same boat to fish in year after year. The superintendent selected the boat the fishermen used. The boats are all constructed the same. Outsiders usually got the best vessels and the newest gear. One season, I received a boat that was built a little narrow in the bow and stern. While fishing for Ekuk, I sailed past many Alaska Packers sailboats, which were also under full sail. The Packer's boats were a bit beamy in the bow and stern, so they were slower. My boat was a dandy; I enjoyed it! I wanted the same boat for the next fishing season, but the superintendent gave me a different boat. It was slower, but it held a few more fish in the stern.

When the wind wasn't blowing furiously, we sailed full sail. If the wind became too strong, the sprit was taken down. Also, part of the sail on the boom was tied. When it was very stormy, the rip tides were respected and even feared. The rips were very choppy, even when there was a slight breeze. In the rips, the waves are close and toss up and down in different directions. These unusually choppy, swirling waves are different than combers, breakers, or ocean swells.

One blustery day, I had to make a fish delivery. Sailing from below Ekuk Bluff, I tacked toward Clark's Point. Once there, my partner threw a line for a tie up alongside an anchored company flat scow. While I was pewing my fish up into the scow, Agafangel, a cousin of mine, sailed up and tied behind me. He hollered that a sailboat capsized at Haller's Spit (this was the spit off Ekuk Cannery, where I sailed a little earlier. It extends straight out from the dock at low water and goes a fair distance). When I heard this, I froze for a

More Sailboat And Other Fishing Stories

moment. I wanted to hear more.

Leaving my work, I moved closer to Agafangel. He said he saw the boat go under. As it turned over, the stacked salmon nets popped to the surface. A fishermen appeared in the turbulent whitewash. With heavy rubber boots and rain gear on, he should have sunk like a stone. Luckily, he was able to make it to the surface and grabbed the tangled mass of corks. Since the strong tide had already turned, the unfortunate victim began to drift quickly downriver. Fortunately, a tug boat captain nearby saw the capsizing. He throttled his vessel. In a few minutes, with his boat tossing crazily, he idled alongside the threatened fishermen. Soon, the gasping man was pulled into the boat. Luckily, the man wasn't hurt during the rescue. The other man who was aboard the capsized vessel disappeared. When the boat overturned, he was pulled under by the powerful current. This accident occurred while I was pewing salmon aboard the tally scow, less than a mile away.

At the closure of fishing that week, I visited my mother, who lived in a house overlooking the beach near Ekuk Cannery. She said that earlier, while she was staring at Nushagak Bay from her window, she saw the heavily loaded sailboat navigating Haller's Spit. The waves were treacherous. From her account, a gigantic, swirling wave rose, broke, and tossed the boat sideways. It hit broadside and rolled completely over. Although saddened by the loss, I knew that drownings occurred. It happens during sudden, strong windstorms, which frequent the area. It would befall usually inexperienced captains who overloaded their sailboats. This was bad judgement.

Another unfortunate event occurred one spring in the mid-1920s. My father was winter watchman for the Alaska Packers Cannery at Clark's Point. As watchman, he was also responsible for launching the tug boat and scow. The vessels were useful for off-loading cannery workers who arrived from Seattle. After launching the Heron, he became the skipper. Dad hired me to work as engineer. He showed me how to start and stop the tug's diesel engine. He also showed me the controls for putting the engine in forward gear and reverse gear. From the pilot house, my father rang a bell signaling me to set the gear in forward, reverse, or neutral. If more communications were needed, there was a tube connected from the pilothouse to the engine room. The captain yelled instructions into the mouthpiece to the engineer below deck. The orders came through clearly.

That spring, as a fifteen-year-old teenager, I worked as Heron's chief engineer. I relinquished this position after the Seattle ship arrived. A more experienced engineer took over. I became the tug boat's deck hand until commercial fishing began. One day, as a deck hand, I helped tie the tug alongside a large sailing ship. After climbing the ladder onto the ship, Dad and I were invited to have lunch in the captain's quarters. When I finished eating, Dad told me to tell the new engineer to come up and eat lunch. I climbed down the ladder, entered the tug's cabin, and jumped down the hatch into the engine room. The engine room smelled like exhaust smoke. Not finding the engineer in the usual place, I noticed him stretched out on the floor. Surprised, I rushed out of the Heron, quickly climbed the ship's ladder, and anxiously told my father the engineer was laying, probably dead, on the Heron's engine room floor.

My father rushed down to the Heron accompanied by a couple other men from the ship. Locating the engineer, they carried him onto the deck. They hoped the fresh air would revive him. In the rush, I forgot to shut off the tug's engine. Later, I did. Soon, the engineer revived. Several hours later, the engineer, feeling better, repaired an exhaust leak.

In the sailing days, there weren't any weekly closed fishing periods. Later, the United States Bureau of Fisheries closed Sundays for commercial fishing. After a few more years, they began closing fishing on Wednesdays. After statehood, the Alaska Department of Fish and Game published open and closed fishing periods, according to the status of the fish run and its escapement goals. Since statehood, you never knew what days you would fish. We had to wait for the announcements from the Fish and Game office.

As a youngster, after a fishing closure, I watched fishermen piling their linen nets into a long, narrow, low tank called the blue stone tank. The nets soaked in the blue stone solution. This took the fish slime out

More Sailboat And Other Fishing Stories

of the net and kept the color in the mesh. Later, when fishermen received nylon salmon gillnets, they were instructed by the superintendent to blue stone their nets every closed period.

At the closure, the fishermen tied their sailboats alongside the cannery dock. The dock had dozens of boats tied up at one time. Soon after arrival, finding a location next to an open piling, they pulled their nets up on the planked wooden dock. The nets were stacked onto a four wheeled, hand-pulled truck. With the truck piled high with gear, they pulled them over to the blue stone tank area. With a fresh water hose, they hosed down their nets. After the initial cleaning, the nets were pulled by hand and piled in the blue-stoned water. They laid in the tanks for about an hour, then they were pulled out and piled on the truck. Next, they were pulled over onto the cannery dock to a freshwater hose and hosed down again. Then, the nets were pulled back down into the fish boats. This work was an inconvenience, but we took it for granted. It was something which had to be done when fishing for the company.

Later, when fishermen became independent and bought their own power boats, they weren't forced to blue stone their own nets. They generally washed their nets with river water forced through the vessel's hydraulic pumps and hoses after the fishing period closed.

Over the years, I had several fishing partners I enjoyed. One partner was an exceptional picker, and fished with me for twelve seasons. His wife was the nurse at Ekuk Cannery. I had another partner for eight seasons. This partner used to work for the beach gang. I managed to have the beach boss agree to let me take him. He was a good man, and after eight seasons, he got his own sailboat. I remember another partner who played the accordion. At almost every fishing closure, we listened to his lively music.

One season, I decided to take my youngest brother, Lawrence. One gusty evening, amidst the white caps, we laid out three, fifty-fathom gillnets on the bottom end of Middle Channel. This was close to the lower Nushagak Bay boundary marker. After watching the corks awhile, we went to sleep. While asleep, we were drifting in on the flood tide toward Ekuk Bluff. The boat keel suddenly hit with such

No Half Truths

force on a sand bar we awoke with a startle. I pulled myself out of the bedding. Peering out of the tent, and looking toward the stern of the boat, I realized we were in danger. It was so rough that waves were smashing into both sides of the boat. Although Lawrence was alongside me, I yelled at him to grab a bucket. Without boots or rain gear on, we bailed furiously. As we were bailing the water out, I was amazed that the wood planks didn't come apart. The boat continued to toss haphazardly. It rose, hesitated, and then fell hard on the sand-covered bar. Lawrence's eyes were huge with fear. He was drenched with cold saltwater. When the boat hit again, especially hard, we hung on for dear life. The boat was hammered several more times less severely. Thankfully, the rising tide currents pushed us (net and all) across the narrow bar. Soon, we were in deeper water. Breathlessly, we inspected the boat for any leaks. Noticing no leaks and after drifting a bit further up the channel, we finally settled down. We changed clothes and went back to sleep.

Lawrence discovered he didn't like sailboat fishing, so he quit after the season. I have to hand it to him for not quitting after that rough fishing period. For years, he kidded me that the reason why he quit was because he couldn't stand the Copenhagen snuff all over the boat.

After I purchased my own conversion, I named it the John W. The name John W was painted over a fresh, gray paint job. With this boat, I became an independent fishermen. I took my sons as partners for several years. Frank, especially, was a good picker.

My son, William, was my partner for a time. Later, when he was sixteen years old, Frank gave him a 22-foot Seamore Skiff. Frank, who was going to college stayed in Ohio to learn the drafting trade that summer. The skiff did not have a motor. William oared and let his net out. When I made a move to a better fishing area, I towed him with the John W. That first season, he did okay. The next season, he convinced the cannery superintendent to purchase an outboard motor. He built a fine wooden roller, which was attached next to the motor on the stern of the skiff.

I always made it a point to keep an eye on him. I told William

More Sailboat And Other Fishing Stories

repeatedly, "Don't lay your nets too far from my boat. You may have motor problems, you may catch too much fish, or a storm may kick up and I can help you."

During a breezy day, we were fishing halfway up Middle Channel. The end of the fishing period was quickly approaching. With apprehension, I was pulling in my nets to beat the closure time. Glancing over at William, I also wondered why he wasn't pulling his nets in. He was about a mile-and-a-half from my boat.

After my buoy was pulled in, I rushed toward his skiff. To my surprise he was helpless! My partner jumped into William's boat and immediately pulled in his nets. William had sprained his back when he tried to pull his nets in. When I began towing his skiff to the Clark's Point Beach, he laid down flat on the bottom of his boat. I radioed ahead for an emergency plane to take him to the Kanakanak Hospital.

Once at Clark's Point Beach, in order to get him out of the skiff, four men placed him on a flat board. He could not move because of the awful pain. The doctor told me later that William had severely sprained his back. He spent a few days in the hospital. When he was released, he went back out fishing again.

Toward the last part of that same fishing season, we were fishing at half tide, near the mud banks at Coffee Point. William laid his nets out a short distance from me. While he was drifting, the current took him out to the rip. Breaking white caps were showing. As I watched his skiff, I began to think the waves might sink him. Soon, he began to pull the net in with a few fish. Worried, I again quickly pulled my fish nets and motored toward him. I bawled him out and asked why he didn't pull his nets in before he got into the tide rip! William seemed to enjoy the rough water. I kept my eye on him for a couple of seasons, then he was on his own. He fished the small skiff for about nine or ten years.

After limited entry, William purchased his first power boat—the Cutty Shark from Dennis Andrew, a Native from New Stuyahok. He fished this wooden boat for a couple of seasons, sold it, then purchased a new thirty-two-foot Rawson boat. This was a fiberglass boat. He named it the Barbara Clare, after his wife. Later, he changed the name

131

to John W. He sold this too, and bought another fiberglass Roberts boat from his friend, Tom Hoseth. It carried more fish, and was a comfortable boat to fish in. It was full of electronics. He named this boat after his son, John W II. The John W II (John W "also"), is currently performing very well as a gillnetter for Togiak herring and Bristol Bay salmon. For a couple of years, in the early 1990s, William also long-lined for halibut in Bristol Bay's small boat halibut nursery area fishery.

Chapter Eighteen

Fishermen Unions

During the sailboat days, there was one fishermen's union to represent fishermen. This union was called the Alaska Fishermen's Union, and was organized on September 26, 1902. After World War Two, two fishermen groups represented fishermen. They were known as the Alaska Fishermen's Union and the Western Alaska Cooperative Marketing Association (WACMA). There were other local unions or associations organized, but they didn't last long. An example was the Snag Point Fishermen's Union, which lasted one year. WACMA represented the local fishermen interests, while Alaska Fishermen's Union usually represented Outside fishermen.

When the Outsiders' union struck and settled salmon prices. We, the local residents, didn't agree on the price, so WACMA continued the strike. Finally succeeding on getting a better price for our salmon, the final difference was two or three cents a fish.

During the late forties, I was on the strike picket line for a few days. We finally got our price settled with the buyers and went fishing. We lost considerable fishing time to get our price. Another time, during the first part of the fifties, WACMA settled on a set price for the salmon, but the Outside fishermen wanted a better price for their fish. During their strike, they wouldn't unload ships anchored offshore, or do any labor onshore.

I fished for Ekuk Cannery. Ekern, the superintendent for the cannery, asked me if I would skipper the power scow named the Mink to unload the ship. I said okay, since this was not perceived as wrong by the local fishermen's group. As captain of the power scow, I towed a flat scow out to the ship. I freighted the cannery supplies to shore and also a big load of coal for the boilers. Just when I had taken all the cannery supplies from the ship to shore, salmon prices for the Outside fishermen got settled for the same price WACMA settled for. At some point, the unions convinced the canneries they should pay one price for salmon. This I always supported.

Fisherman Unions

Strikes were always a difficult time. In the earlier years, when we were on strike, the fishermen meetings seemed to go on and on. Sometimes, several days and/or weeks went by before a settlement was reached. If the strike was not over before the main run, over-escapement occurred on the spawning grounds. Maybe, by letting more fish go by for escapement, it would build up a bigger run for the next cycle, but that's not the way fishermen looked at it.

Dad told me that, in the latter 1800s he'd seen salmon spawn over a foot thick in the Wood River lakes. From statehood on, fisheries management people don't like over-escapement in the rivers and lakes of the region. There is biological harm done on reproduction levels. Economically speaking, fishermen believe that over-escapement does more harm than under-escapement.

Chapter Nineteen

Visit To The Lower Forty-Eight

The first time I left Alaska was in the fall of 1924, at eighteen years of age. I departed the Nushagak area for San Francisco, with the idea of learning a trade. Because of my background, I wound up captaining a small freight scow. I ran the scow piled high with equipment from moored sailing ships at Alaska Packers Shipyard. After a time, I left this job. I finally located an educational opportunity. I began training as a machinist in the Atlas Imperial Engine Works machine shop at Oakland, California. This shop manufactured diesel engines. At the machine shop, I learned to grind engine valves and rocker arms to perfection. Although I tried to keep myself busy, I got very homesick for Alaska. I missed driving my dog team, trapping, and hunting. In the spring of 1925, when I left San Francisco for Nushagak Bay, I said to myself, "I will never go stateside again."

Years later, in 1980, when I was seventy-four years old, I again left my home. The reason I left this time was because my oldest sister,

Emma, who earlier had moved to Sunnyvale, California, was having problems with her eyes. She needed an eye operation. I wanted to see her in case her eyes deteriorated further. With my wife, Bessie, my son, Hans, and his family, I flew to visit Emma. (Hans and his family were headed out to visit their in-laws at Albuquerque, New Mexico.)

We rented an automobile. After first visiting my sister, I drove down to tour Disneyland. We wound up staying one night in Los Angeles. The next day, we visited the playgrounds of Disneyland. That evening, we drove back to Sunnyvale for the night. The next morning, we drove on the Golden Gate Bridge. This was the first time, I'd driven on the bridge. When I was in San Francisco in 1924, the scuttlebutt was that a bridge would be built across the Golden Gate.

After we crossed the Golden Gate Bridge, we drove over to the Oakland Bay Bridge, crossed it and continued to the Upper Bay Bridge and crossed it too. Later, we returned the rental car unit and caught a flight to Albuquerque, New Mexico. My wife and I stayed in Albuquerque for eighteen days. Finally, when we were ready to leave, we caught a flight back to Anchorage and to Kanakanak, which was home sweet home! I found out later that my sister's eyes got better after the operation. The trip was certainly worthwhile.

In the autumn of 1989, I made my third trip stateside. My daughter, June, with her husband, Jay, and their two boys (One was two years old, the other three.) moved from Kanakanak to Topock, Arizona. We immediately missed them, especially since my wife, Bessie, baby-sat the boys ever since they were born. My wife was so attached to the boys, she pestered me. She wanted to see them during the following winter. So, again, I flew out of Alaska in February 1990, at the age of almost eighty-four years.

Leaving Dillingham with Billy Backford, who had a house in San Diego, California, we arrived there, where my son in-law, Jay Hoover, and family met us. We rented a motor home and drove up to Sunnyvale to visit Emma. We took a second look at the Bay bridges (my home in Kanakanak is next to the bay—I like the water), then drove down to the huge city of Los Angeles. The next day, mainly for June's kids, we visited Disneyland. After that, we went to Animal

Visit To The Lower Forty-Eight

World.

The next day, we chartered a vessel off San Diego to watch surfacing and diving whales. Still not tiring of travel, we drove by car to Topock, where my daughter, June, lived. There, June took my wife and I on a tour.

We saw the Grand Canyon, with its huge gorge cut down through the ages. What was interesting before we got there, snow was on the ground. We saw unusual looking arid trees and a few deer. While at the canyon, I purchased a cup and an ash tray. The tray was stamped "Grand Canyon National Park, Arizona". On another day, we went up to the Hoover Dam. While there, we were taken down to the bottom of the dam on the Colorado River.

On my third and last trip stateside, I was gone twenty days before returning to my hometown at Kanakanak. Again, arriving home was sweet. The Lower Forty-eight States may have warmer temperatures, more sunshine, and beautiful trees and flowers, but I will take Bristol Bay anytime!

Chapter Twenty

Marriages

In 1930, I married a young woman named Mary Olson. She was a beautiful, quarter-breed Native. Mary gave birth to three fine children—Florence, Ina, and Edward. What stands out is that, from 1939, for a number of seasons, I took my family by sailboat to Ekuk. I also took nine sled dogs, washing tubs, wringer, cooking utensils, blankets, and mattresses. Our boat was loaded. While I driftnetted by sailboat, my wife setnetted on Ekuk Beach. After fishing was over, I loaded the boat with all of our belongings. With my entire family on board, I sailed toward Kanakanak.

My second marriage occurred in 1950. I married an industrious Eskimo woman from Togiak named Bessie Nugulra. With Bessie and her son, Frank, I traveled to Ekuk each summer with a boat load of gear. Later, with the arrival of three more children—William, Hans, and Jane—I continued this until 1959 with a larger load. In 1960, I decided to fish for PAF, which had a cannery at Dillingham. The cannery was closer to my home, so I didn't have to move my family anymore. My wife, Bessie, quit setnetting at Ekuk Beach, which lessened our income. This was okay.

William graduated from high school in Dillingham in 1969, then, finished both college and graduate school. After fishing each season, he attended Seattle Pacific College (now Seattle Pacific University) in Washington state for two years. Then, for another two years, he attended George Fox College in Oregon, where he receive his B.A. He continued to fish each season. After fishing for another three seasons, he continued and finished his education at the Moravian Theological Seminary. The seminary is located in Bethlehem, Pennsylvania. There, he received a Masters Degree.

In Dillingham, in the fall of 1977, William was ordained as a Moravian minister by Bishop Kortz from Pennsylvania. He officiated at the large Moravian church in Bethel as an interim pastor for one winter. Here, he discovered and married Barbara Mojin, who was originally from Nunapitchuk. After Bethel, he moved back to Dillingham, where he served as a local church pastor. He served successfully at the Dillingham Moravian Church, his home church. The pastor's salary was extremely low at the time, so he continued fishing to support his family.

Like myself, fishing is in William's blood too! Fishing provided good income for him as the commercial fishing industry improved in the late 1970s and early 1980s.

With the extra money he earned, he became interested in dog racing. This brought our families closer together. His mother, Bessie, and his wife, Barbara, split fish to feed the dogs. He raised a team of racing dogs that ran an average of sixteen to eighteen miles an hour. They produced a steady pace for up to twenty two miles without slowing down. In fact, the last mile or two, they ran even faster. He attended most of the major dog races around the region.

The first time he raced, he won a red lantern for the slowest team in the Beaver Roundup Festival, Western Alaska Championship races. Later, with further experience and acquisition of a faster breed of dog, his team was running faster. He won second- and third-place

Marriages

trophies in the yearly championship races. The dogs were expensive to keep, feed, and train, yet very beautiful to look at.

I've always enjoyed dogs and festivities, so I'll say a bit more. The important dog races occur during the Beaver Roundup time during March or April. These races last for three days, and cash prizes for dog races are as high as four to six thousand dollars for first place. The dog races are a central and traditional part of these festivities. They're broadcast by radio so the entire region can listen. During the Beaver Roundup festivities, there are many other events which are enjoyable, such as snowmachine races, parade, rope pulling, a pinochle contest, baking, beauty pageants, and many other activities.

During the 1992 Beaver Roundup smoked fish contest, Barbara won first prize for the best king salmon smoke fish in Bristol Bay. William is proud of his wife's accomplishment. Currently, both William and Barbara have five children—Shawna, age 15, broke the 1995 State Native Youth Olympics seal-hop record, which was held for sixteen years; John W, age 11; Earl, age 4; Jerilyn, age 1; and Parsha, just a couple of months old.

Maybe, I should add another thing—when the Togiak herring fishery began in the late 1970s, William helped to organize the Bristol Bay Herring Marketing Cooperative in fall of 1979. William served as the president of the cooperative. Along with other directors, they invited several Japanese companies from Tokyo, Japan, to purchase gillnet-caught herring. This was the Japanese Longline Gillnet Association.

After a long political battle that ended up in the courts, the co-op secured an internal waters processing permit. This permit allowed them to operate. Through the subsequent creation of a joint venture corporation, it allowed hundreds of local herring fishermen to sell herring. U.S. buyers didn't want gillnet roe caught fish, so the Japanese bought herring from them from 1981 through 1987. In 1988, the American fisheries were totally Americanized. The Japanese buyers were forced to drop out. My son, William, told me he hopes to publish a fish story about the Togiak herring fishery and their experiences with the Japanese buyers. He was also involved in helping to start the experimental Bristol Bay small-boat halibut fishery.

Hans, my younger son, graduated from Dillingham High School. Afterward, he attended the University of Fairbanks for the winter. While there, he experienced a problem with nose bleeds. The air was probably too dry. After he came home, they ceased.

After fishing with me a few seasons in my conversion, Hans purchased a Wagley fiberglass, 32-foot power boat. He named it after his daughter, Jennifer Lynn, who won the 1995 Miss Bristol Bay beauty contest—the region's largest beauty pageant.

Hans fished the Jennifer Lynn a few seasons, until the summer of 1991. In the winter of 1992, he bought an aluminum bowpicker vessel constructed in the state of Washington. This boat has a hydraulic bow roller and reel, which is used to lay out and pull in the gillnet. He has a single-sideband radio powerful enough to talk to San Francisco. With his Echo-tech, he knows where he is at all times in the fishing districts, within a few feet, in foggy weather. The boat cruises over thirty five knots. It has held over forty thousand pounds of herring in one load. My old conversion was lucky to hold up to fifteen hundred fish (eight thousand pounds). This new boat is also named the Jennifer Lynn. Hans fishes for herring at Togiak each spring. In order to store his boat, he recently built a large warehouse at Kanakanak. It's big enough to store two power boats with room to spare.

During the 1992 fishing season, Hans fished the well-publicized, hectic Egegik salmon fishery. His wife, Danesa, and four children, the youngest one seven years old, fished the entire season at Egegik. They did real good down there. It turned out to be the largest recorded catch in history at this district. Hans is a hard-working fisherman, and always does very well.

After fishing is over, he works as a fireman, drives a fuel truck, and does other odd jobs during the winter months. He's vice president of Choggiung, Ltd., our local village corporation, which owns the Bristol Inn. Hans has four children: Jennifer, age 17; Mark, age 16; Robert, age 12; and Ryan, age 9.

Danesa took an Emergency Medical Technician (EMT) course at

Marriages

the University Extension Service in Dillingham. She's on call and rides the ambulance to the hospital. During her training to get her EMT certificate, I invited her over to take my blood pressure. She did this when I was almost eighty-seven years old; she said my numbers were good.

My daughter, Jane, graduated from high school in Dillingham in 1973. While she was going to school here, she was one of a few students who were sent to Europe on an educational trip.

First, she landed in Copenhagen, Denmark, stayed there for two days, then traveled to Spain for three months. While in Spain, she made a side trip to Portugal. There, she had an interesting boat ride on a cruise ship to Morocco, Africa. She visited Morocco for two days, then went back to Spain.

After Jane finished school in Dillingham, she went to business college in Anchorage for nine months. After finishing school, she decided to begin work at Bethel. There, she was employed as a Chief Deputy Clerk and was later promoted to Clerk of the Court. Jane also worked on the Alaska Pipeline from 1975 through 1977 as a part-time secretary and postmistress. Now, she works at the Bristol Bay Housing Authority in the accounting department.

Jane assists her husband, Victor Sifsof, on the fishing boat. She also knows how to drive dog teams competitively. Racing for several years, her best accomplishment was third place during the Western Alaska State Championship sprint races in Dillingham. She and Victor have two growing sons, Victor (VG), age 13; and Bryan, age 15.

June, my adopted daughter, was born in 1965. She graduated from Dillingham High School. After graduation, she began working as a clerk at the N&N Market, a large Dillingham grocery store. Later, she was employed at the National Bank of Alaska, and then switched to work for Nushagak Electric for a better salary. June got married to Jay Hoover and later moved to Arizona. She loves commercial fishing. Each season she comes back to Alaska and fishes as a crew member with my son, William. June is of great help around my home presently, since she moved back with her family to Dillingham in the autumn of 1994. Now, she works as a bank teller at the National Bank of Alaska, Dillingham Branch. She has two boys—Kyle is eight and Jason is ten.

My youngest daughter, April, was born in 1966. While in grade school, she was sent to Hawaii on a school trip. When she arrived back home, she was a little sunburned. Later, she went to Hawaii on her own. She graduated from Dillingham High School in 1984, then took courses of study at the University of Alaska, Anchorage. She was on the basketball team when she attended the university.

April loves snowmachining and hunting ptarmigan. Over the years, she spent a lot of time helping her brother, William, and my son-in-law, Victor, to harness their sled dogs during the Beaver Roundup races.

One time, April joined the races with her own borrowed dog team. The day of the race, the weather was very mild. The creeks were full of water, so she scratched from the races. She didn't want to get wet swimming with the dogs in the creeks. It was a one-day race. As it turned out, other dog mushers dropped out too. It was really a three-day race, but this got canceled, which was very unusual.

April began employment for Choggiung Limited, April 25, 1985, as an accounting clerk. She is doing quite well. She is now a bookkeeper. She is married to Adolf "Buddy" Roehl, a member of the Alaska Army National Guard. Buddy comes from a large family in Dillingham. They have one child, a daughter named Erin, aged one year old.

One day, about seven years ago, Hans asked me if I would return his skiff from his fishing boat anchored offshore at Kanakanak Creek. I never had any real experience with modern outboard motors. He ran the skiff out to the boat. Leaving Hans there, I took control of the skiff motor and began heading back to shore. Just a few feet from my son's boat, the motor quit. I tried to start the motor in low throttle, but it wouldn't start. I advanced the throttle as far as it would go and pulled the starting chord. The motor erupted into life. It instantly propelled the skiff forward, and I lost my balance and fell. I wasn't holding the steering handle, so the skiff rapidly went round and round in a circle!

I was very lucky I didn't fall overboard. As soon as I got up and got my balance, breathless, I slowed the throttle, steered the skiff to shore, and beached it.

My grandson, Robert, who was seven years old then, was watching me on the beach. When he arrived at his home up on the hill, overlooking Kanakanak Creek, he told his mother. My wife soon heard that, "Grandpa was going round and round, round and round in the skiff out in the water." The way I later heard his story, shared by his grandmother, Bessie, was comical.

Chapter Twenty One

Skating At 84 Years Of Age

During the winter of 1989, I was watching excited people who were enjoying ice skating at the Dimond Mall Ice Rink in Anchorage. My daughter, Jane, was sitting next to me. I startled her when I said I wanted to go skating too. She looked at me and said, "If you do, you'll break your neck!"

The last time I had skates on was when I was twenty one years old—about sixty three years earlier. When my Jane and a few relatives left to shop in the mall, I decided I was going to skate. I rented a pair of ice skates and put them on. I hobbled onto the ice. Much to my surprise, I could still skate. Although I was eighty four years old, my feet still obeyed my mind. Soon, my relatives came back. With their faces showing astonishment, they scrutinized my skating.

I moved through a crowd of children and other young adults at the Dimond Ice Rink. I quickly skated near them, took off my hat, and bowed a little. Grinning, I skated away. Over the last several years, I have skated several times at the Dimond Skating Rink. I imagine, because of my age, I received attention in the press. I also received a letter from the Governor of Alaska for my skating exploits. I hung his letter on my living room wall, along with other awards.

When I was a teenager, I fabricated my own skates from a block of wood and a flat piece of iron. When winter arrived and ice on the ponds was thick enough, my brothers and I went ice skating. Generally, we didn't have much time to skate, because as soon as the ice was solid enough, it began to snow. When it snowed, it was the end of ice skating for the year.

For those concerned about old brittle bones, I must be truthful. The first time I rented skates, they were figure skates. These skates had some teeth in front on the blade. I didn't know this when I hurriedly tied the shoe laces. At first, I hesitated on the ice. I then carefully pushed myself out on the rink. In a short while, I began to skate quite well. When I raised up my heel a little, the teeth grabbed the ice. I fell forward on the rink—flat on my face! After that, I was well acquainted with figure skates. I became very cautious. Thankfully, so far, I haven't had a bad fall.

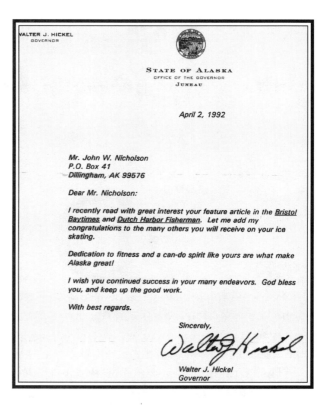

Chapter Twenty Two

Alcoholic Days

Drinking alcohol has always been a problem in Bristol Bay. Countless fishermen drowned through accidents associated with drinking. It became so bad, canneries ordered no drinking was allowed during the sailboat fishing season. Alcohol was present during social events. Trappers were gone all winter. When they arrived before the fishing season, their thirst needed quenching. They spent weeks drinking themselves silly. I also succumbed to strong drink.

Gambling and drinking go together. When the fishing season was over, the setnet and drift fishermen received their settlements. At this time money, was plentiful. As a result, there were always nightly, high-stakes card games going on. I sat in on some small games. Sometimes I won a little money. I also lost a little. Poker continued nearly every night for almost two months at Ekuk alone.

One evening, free drinks were being passed around while I was playing poker. I got pretty drunk. Soon with liquor-driven courage,

I was playing on the side and betting high spade. I did this with at least one hundred to one hundred fifty dollars at a time. This was a lot of money for a fisherman. I continued this every time the cards were dealt around.

At that one game alone, I lost nearly all my summer's wages. Luckily I was single at the time. Losing that money ended my plans for a winter in Anchorage. Importantly, losing all that money, especially when I was drunk, taught me a lesson. After that, I decided to never play poker again, especially with money I needed for winter months. The only gambling I did after that was rummy or pinochle at fifty cents to a dollar a game.

Another fall, I worked at the Ekuk Cannery performing odd jobs until the middle of November. When the job ended, I decided to catch a plane to Anchorage, where I thought I might find work. In Anchorage, I went to a bar on Fourth Avenue. After feeling pretty good from several drinks and feeling no pain, I promenaded down to the railroad yard to look for work. On the way down, I met two men walking out of the railroad grounds. They asked me what I was doing there.

I said, "I'm looking for work!"

They told me there were no job openings.

This didn't stop me. I felt I had nothing to lose, so I entered the railroad office building. Seeing a pleasant-faced man behind the counter, I went up and leaned over the counter. Staring at him in the face and being a bit loud, I said, "I'm a Bristol Bay fisherman, and I'm looking for work!"

When I mentioned Bristol Bay fisherman, the man smiled and said he knows most fishermen from the area are handy, all-around workers. He looked at me intently. After a moment, he asked if I had ever worked on a pile driver.

I said, "Sure, I worked on a pile driver before!" I added, "I drove piling at the Ekuk Cannery dock at Nushagak Bay."

He responded, "Good! Will you be ready to board a plane for Seward tomorrow morning?"

I left a bit cocky. Soon, I was driving piling on a Seward dock.

Alcoholic Days

When this was done, I went out on the railroad tracks. There, I repaired tracks and railroad bridge supports. At that job, I worked about four-and-one-half months. When the work was finished, I rode back to Anchorage. I remained there for a while, and then flew back to Dillingham. Not long after, I made it back to Ekuk for spring work.

Prior to the thirties, most of the larger villages had dance halls called "qasgit." Some of the dances had people who were intoxicated. One evening, during the first World War, I noticed a little wooden keg of home brew stored inside a sled basket. I saw this while traveling by dog team. Several dog teams driven by Natives were traveling from Nushagak to Clark's Point to attend a dancing event. After traveling a short distance, two of the drivers took turns drinking. They drank straight out of the barrel. Natives called this barrel "piivaq." The term was probably derived from a Russian name. After taking a few swigs, they continued on their way. When the keg was empty, a thick mass of flour was left on the bottom. Later, the barrel was cleaned out for the next batch of home brew.

When some Native dances were in full swing, someone laid a bolt of gingham or calico cloth on the hallway floor. While the frolicker is dancing, he or she is pulled onto the main floor area by the cloth.

Seen all over the dance hall floor are expensive guns, newly made snowshoes, traps, clothes made of fur, agutaq (Native ice cream made out of salmon and black berries), and many other items. All of the gifts were danced away by Natives, who gave the gifts to everyone gathered in the dance hall. This was almost like Christmas time. Actually, this custom died because of missionary influences.

During Prohibition in the thirties, many made their own home brew. The whiskey they concocted was called moonshine. Beer was made with hops. The Natives in the area manufactured their own version of home brew with graham flour and sugar.

There was a lot of bootlegging activity during Prohibition. Many deaths resulted from freezing during the winter or drownings in summer. Prohibition was abolished when Roosevelt became President of the United States. Although, I drank, I noticed that when Prohibition was eliminated, there was less crime and deaths associ-

No Half Truths

ated with alcohol. Abolishment was better because there were less criminals around. It also helped the U.S. government to raise taxes, with which to do good.

Through the years, I developed a reputation as a number-one drinker in Dillingham. By the case, I drank whiskey and beer without stopping for weeks. During this time, some longtime drinkers said they didn't remember what they said or did. I thought they were lying. I always remembered almost everything—even when I was very drunk. Finally, when I was middle-aged, and when I became heavily intoxicated, blackouts occurred. I became a believer that the old timers were telling the truth.

Among the local people, ghost stories were numerous. The Natives had many tales to tell. The Native name for ghost is "carayak." When I was a kid, many believed in ghosts. A young person earnestly told me that he had seen a ghost, but I joked about this. I told him that I didn't believe in ghosts. Actually the man, and other Natives scared of the dark, imagined they saw apparitions.

Like a lot of the other superstitious kids, I was little unsure of the dark too. As an adult, I felt I was a ghost buster. However, one day, after drinking liquor and sleeping, something happened. I had a shaky, large-sized spring bed, which I pushed against a big window in my Kanakanak home. While I was sleeping, I saw a white apparition jump through the window. It landed on top of my stomach. Suddenly, in a dreamlike state, I woke up. I noticed my bed was shaking. Later, when I was wide awake, I dismissed this experience as a bad dream.

My first wife, Mary, who remained with me for twelve-and-one-half years, warned me about my drinking habit. The last five years of our relationship, she said if I didn't quit drinking, she was going to leave me. Not paying any attention, finally she did leave and won a divorce settlement.

Single for the next several years, I decided to get married again. Women I courted said I had a problem with drinking. They basically said, "Sorry, you drink too much!" Later, I married a Native widow, Bessie Nugulra, who had a four-year-old boy, Frank. She knew I

Alcoholic Days

drank, but through some of my Native friends, they convinced her I was a good provider.

Bessie endured my drinking bouts for about five years, and then she left me. Not being able to stand loneliness, after a couple months, I went looking for her. She made me promise that I wouldn't drink too much. I promised her I would try. Knowing I needed help, I spoke with a Seventh Day Adventist minister, who tried to help me to quit the habit. He visited nearly every day. Most of the time, I was half drunk, but he finally got me to pray to the Lord Jesus Christ. Finally, after a period of several months, my prayers began to work on my heart and life. Gradually, I cut down and quit completely. I have been married to Bessie for forty five years, and I haven't touched alcohol for forty years.

I believe strongly, if someone is an alcoholic like I was (or has a drug problem), he or she ultimately needs God's help to quit their drinking habit. I also believe anybody who refrains from alcohol for two weeks or so can quit drinking on their own, if they want to. Importantly, they must also commit themselves to stay away from friends who drink.

As an alcoholic, every time I got a cut or scratch, it became infected. Since abstinence, my cuts don't get infected.

I chewed snuff for thirty years. Locals used to joke about me. "Look at your face. Snuff is running down your face!" I must've looked awful during the drinking bouts when snuff ran down my lips and chin. I quit chewing snuff for about twenty seven years. The snuff habit was hard to quit. After quitting, for about two years, I habitually and impulsively reached down in my pockets looking for that snuff can. No more!

Lastly, a message for those combating alcohol. There is always hope for a better life. It made a difference in my life and family. I encourage you to refrain from drinking alcohol. Alcohol is a remover of many things: it is a disinfectant; it is a cleaner; it takes the stain off your clothes; and it removes reputations. A good reputation is better than gold. Not consuming alcoholic beverages helps you to get ahead in life.

Index

A

Abbie	56, 57
Alaska Commercial Company	17
Alaska Department of Fish and Game	31, 121, 122, 128
Alaska Packers	14, 21, 67, 70, 71, 126
Alaska Packers Shipyard	137
Alaska Territorial Guard	107
Alcohol	114, 151, 154, 155
Aleknagik	61, 104, 122
Aleut	66
Anchorage	18, 42, 60, 69, 82, 92, 101, 104, 110, 138, 145, 146, 149, 152, 153
April	8, 13, 27, 38, 41, 45, 50, 78, 88, 94, 105, 117, 143, 146
Atlas Engine Works	68, 137
Auction	32

B

Backford, Billy	138
Banana	17, 18
Barbara	94, 131, 142, 143
Beauty Creek	29, 30
Beaver	7, 37, 38, 39, 40, 41, 42, 43, 84, 85, 142, 143, 146
Beaver Roundup	85, 142, 143, 146
Belanca	41
Bessie	41, 78, 83, 94, 95, 96, 138, 141, 142, 147, 154, 155
Bethel	22, 49, 69, 142, 145
Big Foot's Hill	30
Bishop Kortz	142
Black Slough	41
Bradsford Creek	25, 26, 53
Brailer	81, 120, 121
Bristol Bay	1, 7, 8, 13, 16, 29, 35, 42, 49, 63, 64, 69, 70, 82, 8, 90, 101, 105, 106, 116, 120, 124, 126, 132, 139, 143, 144, 145, 151, 152
Bristol Bay Herring Marketing	82, 143
Bryan	145
Buddy Adolf Roehl	94, 146
Bureau of Fisheries	31, 116, 122, 123, 128
Byron	93

C

Cabin Fever	26, 50
California	9, 47, 68, 89, 106, 137, 138
Caribou	7, 111
Carmel	14, 33
Choggiung	28, 94, 144, 146
Christopher	92
Clark, John W.	17, 66
Clark, Natalia	16
Clark's Point	7, 13, 14, 17, 21, 22, 23, 25, 27,50, 51, 52, 97, 113, 115, 122, 126, 127, 131, 153
Coffee Point	37, 116, 131
Corn flakes	17
Cranberries	53

156

Creek Cannery 52
Cub 41, 102, 103

D

Danesa 93, 144
Davis, Mike 88
Dean 92
Denmark 13, 66, 145
Dentist 18
Dillingham 1, 7, 23, 25, 27, 28, 29, 33, 34, 35, 37, 38, 39, 47, 49, 50, 52, 60, 61, 63, 64, 65, 69, 75, 82, 85, 93, 97, 103, 104, 107, 109, 110, 111, 116, 121, 123, 138, 141, 142, 144, 145, 146, 153, 154
Dimond Mall 149
Doctor Romig 33
Dog Team 7, 15, 22, 26, 27, 37, 38, 39, 40, 41, 43, 49, 51, 52, 53, 54, 55, 56, 57, 76, 77, 86, 102, 103, 137, 146, 153
Dog teams 41, 42, 49, 50, 56, 145, 153
Dollies 122
Dolly Varden 122, 123
Donna 91
Dragnet Cannery 60
Dragnet Seafood 52

E

Earl 94
Egegik 50, 64, 144
Eileen 92
Ekern 134
Ekuk 14, 15, 16, 18, 21, 31, 32, 45, 46, 50, 51, 67, 74, 76, 79, 97, 113, 116, 117, 118, 120, 121, 122, 125, 126, 127, 129, 134, 141, 142, 151, 152, 153
Ekuk Beach 31, 141, 142
Ekuk Bluff 113, 126, 129
Ekuk Cannery 32, 50, 76, 79, 113, 116, 117, 118, 120, 125, 126, 127, 129, 134, 152
Ekuk Church 113
Elizabeth 41, 89
Elmer 41, 69, 101, 102, 103, 104
Emma 9, 16, 66, 89, 138
Erin 94, 146
Ernest 60, 125

F

Federal Marshal 32
Feodora 17, 41, 65
Florence 39, 91, 141
Fordson 59
Fort Alexander 16, 17
Fox 22, 26, 30, 37, 56, 84, 142
Foxes 22, 30, 43
Fur-bearing 41, 42, 68, 107

G

Golia, Andrew 82
Goodnews Bay 49, 111
Grand Canyon 139
Grandfather 17
Grandfather Clark 17
Grandma 16, 17, 50, 51, 73
Grandma Clark 17, 50, 51, 73
Grandmother 16, 17, 18, 147
Grandpa 147
Grassy Island 25, 47, 123
Groat, Sonny 63

H

Hall	51
Hans	13, 18, 61, 65, 79, 84, 93, 104, 138, 141, 144, 146
Hansen, Paul	82
Harvey	88, 91
Hatfield, Fred	38
Herbert	69, 104
Hesse William A.,	60
Hickel, Walter	8
High-Powered	31
Hoidahl, Hans	18
Hoover, Jay	92, 138, 145

I

Ina	39, 92, 141
Iowithla	37, 38, 40, 43

J

Jane	61, 84, 93, 141, 145, 149
Jason	92, 146
Jennifer	93, 144
Jennifer Lynn	144
Jerami	92
Jerilyn	94
John W	1, 7, 13, 17, 66, 94, 96, 130, 132, 143
John W. Nicholson	7
Judge Wickersham	33
June	35, 78, 84, 92, 138, 139, 145

K

Kanakanak	8, 18, 22, 23, 25, 26, 27, 29, 30, 33, 34, 35, 37, 39, 40, 41, 47, 52, 53, 55, 57, 59, 60, 61, 63, 64, 78, 81, 95, 97, 101, 102, 103, 107, 131, 138, 139, 141, 144, 146, 147, 154
Kanakanak Beach	40, 47, 78, 103
Kanakanak Hospital	18, 25, 34, 35, 55, 59, 61, 63, 64, 103, 131
Kanatak	27, 49, 50
Kathy	90
Kayak	39, 45, 97
KDLG	121
Kelly, Paul	82
Kevik, Steve	37
Kicker	40, 52
King, Bob	88
Klondike Creek	30
Klondike Hill	30
Klutak	32, 38
Knowles, Tony	88
Kodiak	27, 30, 64
Koggiung	27, 50
Kulukuk	26, 27, 49, 55, 56, 57, 109
Kuskokwim	22, 33, 111
Kvichak	27, 28, 116, 126
Kyle	92, 146

L

Lake Clark	17
Lawrence	41, 90, 129, 130
Lewis Point	38, 39, 54
Libby	29, 67, 71, 126
Lily Pond	103, 104
Lower Forty-eight	15, 50, 70, 106, 139
Lowes, J.C.	50
Lysol	64

M

Mailboat	49, 50
Manokotak	42, 56, 57
Mark	93, 144
Martha	90
Mary	39, 41, 75, 141, 154
Masters Degree	142
McGill, Joe	82
Mildred	41, 72, 75, 89
Mittendorf	17, 51, 57
Mojin, Barbara	142
Monkey boat	115
Moose	7
Moravian	33, 34, 75, 142
Moravian Mission	14, 33
Moravian Theological Seminary	142
Morgan's, Ed	57
Mulchatna	26, 32

N

Naknek	28, 49, 50, 63, 64, 82
Natalia	16
Nelsonville	52, 101, 109
New Stuyahok	42, 131
Nicholson Air Service	69
Nicholson, Elmer	101
Nicholson, Hans	13, 61, 104
Nicholson, William	9, 61, 104
Nushagak	7, 14, 15, 16, 17, 21, 22, 25, 26, 29, 32, 33, 38, 39, 40, 50, 51, 52, 54, 56, 57, 73, 97, 101, 103, 111, 112, 113, 116, 122, 123, 126, 127, 129, 137, 145, 152, 153
Nushagak Bay	7, 14, 15, 21, 25, 33, 52, 57, 101, 103, 112, 113, 116, 122, 123, 126, 127, 129, 137, 152

O

Oakland	68, 106, 137, 138
Olsen, Ernest	60
Olson, Ernest	125
Olson, Mary	141
O'Neil, Ray	82
Owens, Johnny	57

P

Pacific American Fisheries	29, 71, 116
PAF	29, 116, 123, 141
Parsha	94
Peter Pan Seafood	29
Pew	23, 115, 121
Pewing	81, 115, 120, 126, 127
Pile Driver Creek	52
Pile-driver	52
Piper Cub	41, 101
Ptarmigan	7, 16, 27, 41, 46, 47, 48, 51, 53, 54, 146

Q

Qasgiq	97, 98
Queen Slough	27, 28, 50, 52

R

Raven, Emma	9
Raven, Nick	89
Reindeer	27, 38, 40, 43, 57, 109, 110, 111, 112
Road Commission	59, 60

Robert   35, 93, 132, 144, 147
Robin   91
Ronald   92
Ronald Jr.   92
Russian Orthodox Church   16, 73, 74
Ryan   93, 144

S

Salazar, Margaret   28
Samuelsen, Harvey   70, 88, 91
San Francisco   16, 89, 105, 106, 137, 138, 144
Seattle   14, 35, 48, 49, 105, 112, 127, 128, 142
Sharon   90
Shawna   94
Sifsof, Bill   74
Sifsof, Jane   61
Sifsof, Victor   85, 93, 104, 145
Skate   89, 149, 150
Skating   8, 89, 149, 150
Skiff   15, 38, 39, 40, 47, 52, 81, 130, 131, 146, 147
Skyler   92
Smelt   54, 57, 123
Snag Point   28, 47, 50, 52, 59, 60, 63, 97, 103, 111, 133
Snake Lake   102
Snake River   13, 14, 37, 115
Snowmachine   41, 42, 73, 143
Snuff   19, 122, 130, 155
South Forty-eight   106
Spanish Flu   33
Squaw Creek   29, 30, 33, 104
Steve   1, 9, 37, 38
Sunnyvale   9, 138
Swede Stove   114

T

Takaoka   82
Taxi   63, 64, 72, 103, 104
Teeth   18, 19, 150
Ten Day Creek. 57
Territorial Commissioner   31
Territorial School   60
Togiak   26, 49, 55, 56, 57, 82, 104, 132, 141, 143, 144
Trapped   38, 41, 42, 84
Trapping   22, 26, 37, 39, 40, 41, 42, 43, 56, 68, 99, 107, 118, 137
Tripod trail   50
Tundra   14, 26, 38, 40, 41, 43, 51, 53, 101, 103, 109, 110, 111
Typhoid   64

V

VG   93, 145
Victor   85, 93, 104, 145, 146

W

WACMA   88, 133, 134
Walaka, John   72
William   9, 18, 54, 60, 61, 76, 82, 84, 86, 94, 104, 130, 131, 132, 141, 142, 143, 145, 146
Willow Tree Cutoff   60
Windmill Hill   52
Wolf 43
Wood River   25, 32, 41, 43, 52, 54, 60, 111, 112, 113, 122, 135
World War Two   37, 103, 106, 107, 133